ISLAND GIRL

From Orphan to Military Wife

Jackie Musie

Island Girl: From Orphan to Military Wife
Text © 2021 by Jackie Muise
ISBN 978-1-77366-076-9

All rights reserved.

Designed by Cassandra Aragonez
Editing by Lee Ellen Pottie and Richard Lemm
Printed in Canada by Marquis

Library and Archives Canada Cataloguing in Publication

Title: Island girl: from orphan to military wife / Jackie Muise.
Names: Muise, Jackie, author.
Identifiers: Canadiana (print) 20210237961 | Canadiana (ebook)
20210238356 | ISBN 9781773660769
(softcover) | ISBN 9781773660776 (HTML)

Subjects: LCSH: LeBlanc, Mary Elizabeth, 1930-2017. | LCSH: Military
spouses—Maritime Provinces—Biography. | LCSH: Mothers—Maritime
Provinces—Biography. | LCSH: Orphans—Maritime Provinces—
Biography. | LCSH: Maritime Provinces—Biography. | LCGFT:
Biographies. Classification: LCC FC2624.1.L43 M85 2021 | DDC
971.5/03092—dc23

The publisher acknowledges the support of the Government of Canada,
the Canada Council for the Arts and the Province of Prince Edward
Island for our publishing program.

Canada Council Conseil des Arts
for the Arts du Canada

P.O. Box 22024
Charlottetown, Prince Edward Island
C1A 9J2
Acornpress.ca

ACORNPRESS

TABLE OF CONTENTS

FOREWORD

Whenever I am down home to Pictou, Nova Scotia, I always go to the 11:15 A.M. Mass at the Stella Maris Catholic Church. Every Sunday, Dad and I, along with anyone else around at the time and feeling the urge, can be seen perched there, right side, mid-section. The "dine and dashers" my Aunt Leenie calls us, as immediately after every Communion, we hustle down the side aisle, past our seats, and straight out the front door. Through years of summer vacations, holidays and other special occasions, and hundreds of rushed weekends, rarely have we deviated from that Sunday place and time.

That is, until a drizzling cold day in April 2017, one that gripped the final fringes of a seemingly endless Nova Scotia winter. On that Sunday, Dad and I went to an earlier Mass at a different church, a few minutes' drive from the Palliative Care Unit of New Glasgow's Aberdeen Hospital. Inside the century-old Our Lady of Lourdes in Stellarton, surrounded by rows of darkly stained pews and pale green walls, we found our way to an empty spot near the front left. There we knelt, both of us praying, we confessed to each other, for an end to her pain and release from the agony of watching her suffer. Still, when it happened, we were not ready.

The previous fall 2016, Mary LeBlanc, my mother, and Dad's wife and life partner of sixty-five years, was diagnosed with terminal pancreatic cancer, a cruel pronouncement, coming only two and a half months after the death of my oldest brother, Bob, their first-born. Time was short, said the specialist in Halifax. Mum was a frail eighty-six years old, and the disease already three months advanced. Mumbling our thanks to the disappearing lab coat, we gathered our hats and coats and returned to Pictou for the at home management plan. Whatever was needed, they said, nursing support, equipment, pain control, and, if necessary, twenty-four-hour professional care on the palliative unit: a peaceful passing medically assured.

Mum had different ideas. Weeks stretched to months as she battled against the heavy narcotics, determined to handle the spiraling pain and the crippling disease on her own terms. Christmas came and went, the first without Bob, followed by another three months of plunging and rebounding, in-and-out of whatever hospital bed and unit happened to be available—the system not quite able to deliver what was, in theory, the best of palliative plans.

Yet, while Nova Scotia Health may be forgiven, we, her family, should have known better. Despite her naturally tiny stature and the ever-endearing exterior she chose to present to the outside world, inside was a rod of steel. She was a fighter. From the beginning, life had given her few other options.

Mum aboard the Italia on
the way to Germany

1

SOURIS, PEI, 1930s

Less than a year into the Great Depression, after Wall Street's stock market crash in 1929, times were turbulent for most of the industrialized world. For the people of Canada's smallest province, Prince Edward Island, however, cries that the sky was falling were distant and faint. During the early part of that long decade, life on the Island carried on in much the same way it had for a hundred years before, firmly tied to an economy coaxed out of red soil and pulled from blue-grey seas. Coal, lumber, and other essential supplies were often stretched and made to do. Cash was already scarce comparatively and Islanders commonly measured success by a solid roof, heat in the winter, food on the table, and the occasional opportunity for a tune and dance.

Still, some people did eventually fall to the dreaded dole, especially from the bigger, more commercialized towns. In the spring of 1930 the seaside community of Souris, population about one thousand at the time, was solidly considered one of those towns. Souris sits beside a long coastal indent on the northeastern tip of PEI, where the Gulf of the St. Lawrence sweeps around the eastern coast, in a perpetual wind, to meet the Northumberland Strait. The Anglophones once called it Mouse Harbour, but the Acadian name stuck, as did the Acadians, and the town flourished based on everything that was "Islander": farming, fishing, commercial porting, and shipbuilding in its day.

West and East Souris, as it was known then, mirrored the whole of Prince Edward Island with rolling farmlands inland, and was guarded by the Souris East Lighthouse, a giant sentinel on jagged red rock fourteen meters above the harbour and the Îles de la Madeleine ferry terminal. Some days, Nova Scotia's Cape Breton Highlands appeared clearly on the horizon.

Mary Elizabeth Whitty was born on March 8, 1930, by midwife, in the Souris East Lighthouse. At that time the Souris Lighthouse keeper was Francis McIntosh, Sr., who resided with his family in the living quarters attached to the lighthouse, which was, in fact, a two-story home with four large rooms upstairs, a long narrow kitchen downstairs, a cold room, a small sitting room, and a tiny parlour. At one point, there were as many as twenty-one people living there, including Frank McIntosh's immediate and extended family.

In the beginning, they called her Elizabeth, often shortened to "Lizzie." She was tiny, thin, and small-boned. Her fine dark hair was naturally straight and framed her fair, round face, high cheek bones, sharp nose, and small hazel eyes, the left one weakened slightly whenever she was tired or emotions were high.

Elizabeth was not the daughter of Frank and his wife Christina. That much she knew. She also knew that her biological mother, her "real" mother, lived with her in the lighthouse. Beyond that, images from her early childhood were milky and fleeting, with an enduring sense that other children lived there and, that it was, thoroughly, Mrs. McIntosh's house.

Frank McIntosh Sr.'s official tenure as the Souris East Lighthouse keeper lasted until late 1935. That same year, about a month after Elizabeth's fifth birthday, Rudolph and Jeannette Gallant, a farming couple from St. Georges, about twenty miles south of Souris, arrived at the McIntosh home. The Gallants had not met the McIntoshes, and so the visit was conducted formally. The Gallants were received, not in the kitchen, but in the rarely used parlour off the front entrance. Jeannette Gallant was her usual social self that day, pleasant and talkative, perhaps a little overly so; her husband, Dolph, was quiet and reserved. They accepted a cup of tea and a small refreshment, but stayed only long enough to rest and water the horse. At the end of the brief visit, the couple left and took Lizzie with them. The Gallants had three boys and no girls, and Lizzie was going to live with them on their farm. She would be a great help to Mrs. Gallant.

Teresa, one of the McIntoshes' younger daughters, was nearly three years older than Lizzie, and carried the memory of that day her entire life. "We had lived together all our childhood until then," she said many decades later. "The people who came for her had a buggy, I remember. You know, the one-horse trap with the big wheels and wide bench. Course, they didn't need anything bigger. It was sad, that's why I remember."

The round trip from St. Georges to Souris was a full-day excursion for the Gallants, ending well past bedtime at the small two-bedroom farmhouse on a hill. Elizabeth had her own room readied, at the top of a narrow staircase in the only female exclusive space available, the attic. It contained a single wood-framed bed with a homemade quilted mattress and a brown two-drawer bureau that fit snuggly under the window between the sloped walls. The window faced east, with plenty of light at sunrise.

Initially, Elizabeth stayed close to Jeannette and one-year-old Charlie, who was still semi-attached to Jeannette's hip. She was quiet, Jeannette observed those first days, weeks, and months, doing her best to ingratiate herself, her role as helper carried out as

3

earnestly as a five-year-old could manage. Mostly she entertained Charlie. As the seasons changed, Elizabeth gradually moved beyond the soft, warm cushion that was Jeannette and her kitchen, to the back step, to the yard, and made her way to the wood and wired henhouse, drawn by the chickens and the boys who stole their eggs and made them squawk. The coop stood off the ground on spindly stilts to protect against burrowing predators and was surrounded by a dusty yard about fifty metres from the back door.

As an adult, Elizabeth had no concrete memory of those early days, her recollections a blend of what she had been told through the years and her subconscious. She was certain, though, that she did not ask anyone why she had to leave the lighthouse.
For Elizabeth, the only question was why didn't her real mother come too?

2

LIFE IN ST. GEORGES

Jeannette (Delorie) Gallant was twenty years old in 1922, the year Prince Edward Island granted the provincial vote to women, four years behind Nova Scotia and three years after New Brunswick. The federal female right to vote had been declared earlier by Ottawa, in 1918, after intense pressure by women all over the country who had stepped up for the homeland in the absence of husbands, fathers, and sons during those long and lean First World War years. Canadian women had proven their mettle, and they were not going back.

Change, however, came slowly to the Island and often arrived weakened, having travelled from central Canada, through the Maritime mainland, across the Northumberland Strait, finally fanning itself out like a slow-rolling fog to the rural reaches of PEI.

Soldiers from PEI had also done their part at the sharp end for the war effort, but Island women were accustomed to running their lives and families while their men were at sea or away at winter lumber camps or, in this case, fighting Germans in Europe. In general, most Islanders felt no compulsion to change the status quo regarding so-called women's rights, and so Jeannette, an unmarried woman in her twenties, was considered dangerously close to spinsterhood.

Jeannette was a farmer's daughter, one of ten siblings in a typically big Catholic family from the picturesque eastern inland community of Brudenell, situated between the Montague and

5

Brudenell Rivers. She was average height, a couple inches over five feet, with a prominent nose that precluded her from being described as a typically pretty woman. She did have waving auburn hair, however, bright blue eyes, and a lean and sturdy frame. She was also quick to a song and dance, with a zest for socializing at every opportunity.

Jeannette Delorie was a simple Island woman, uncomplicated in her temperament and emotions, content with the bounty of every day, with activities and people who brought her joy. For Rudolph Gallant she was the embodiment of all that he had been seeking, and had all but given up hope of ever finding. On the day of their wedding in 1927, Jeannette was twenty-five years old, precisely half her new husband's age.

The couple met in Souris where Jeannette was living with her aunt after both her parents passed. She was young when her parents died, eight years old according to provincial archives. More than a century after her birth, Jeannette's early life prior to marriage seems to exist only through those few official documents. Even after she married, Jeannette's personal history was viewed and passed along through the lens of who she was for other people, a wife, mother and grandmother, living in the shadow of a worldly, complicated older man.

Some of that, of course, was in keeping with the dynamics of their times and the limited roles for women during her era. Some of it was Jeannette herself. She was one of those people who loved others without effort and was loved effortlessly in return, whose true value was easily taken for granted, and whose pervasive influence was never fully appreciated.

After Jeannette and Dolph married, they settled down to run their farm in St. Georges and made up for a late start by pro-

6

ducing three boys in quick order. Seven-year-old Joseph was the oldest when Elizabeth arrived, followed by Peter, the same age as Elizabeth. Charles was the baby.

Elizabeth took her designated role as "the girl" seriously, fiercely determined to cement that place. Taking her cue from the boys, she referred to Jeannette as Mum immediately. However, in a remarkably short period of time, with the easy gift that was Jeannette, she really did become Elizabeth's mother in all the ways that simple word implied. As Elizabeth grew, Jeannette would also become the woman Elizabeth aspired to be.

Elizabeth was not that person, though, and never could completely muster the domestic perfection that Jeannette represented: the compliant, doting female, the ever-patient mother and wife. For Elizabeth, reality required regular suspensions of one or more of those attributes, beginning with keeping the lid on a trio of daring and willful farm boys. It soon became apparent that if Elizabeth was to hold her own among them, she would have to help with their management in her own way. Jeannette was a sweet softie, and the boys ran her easily, at least out of earshot and reach of their father.

It was with Dolph, or "the old man" as the boys referred to him, that Elizabeth was having the most difficulty. Frankly, she was afraid of him. Dolph was surly, gruff, and often ill-tempered, and she knew the boys feared him too. What she did not know yet was that her brothers' fear of their father was far healthier than the kind that Elizabeth harboured early on. The boys were fully aware of and, for the most part, respected Dolph's hard boundaries, but they never felt so completely stifled that they avoided interacting with him, nor did his rough manner totally check their propensity to get into trouble. The boys had grown up with the knowledge

7

that Dolph's outward personality did not accurately reflect who he was on the inside. Elizabeth would have to experience and learn that for herself. She did, eventually, but it took several months even to begin the process, which started at a late evening supper that first fall.

Seconds after a flung fork bounced off Peter's forehead and clattered onto the table's dishes, Peter clapped a hand to his puffing eyebrow and shrieked that Elizabeth, unprovoked, had purposely hit him. Across the table, Joe looked at the little girl, now forkless and staring into her plate, and thought the whole thing was hysterically funny, which, of course, sent Peter into a full crying rage. Jeannette hustled to settle him down with a cold cloth, while eighteen-month-old Charlie crashed a bowl of mashed potatoes and deboned mackerel upside down on the floor.

"Cripes all-goddamn-mighty," Dolph finally bellowed, the table's remaining contents lifting with a fist-bang.

"Quiet!"

Dolph was tired. A few minutes' peace at supper shouldn't be too much to expect. It had been a long day and there was still feed to spread and manure to shovel—stuffing it in at one end, troweling the results at the other, a fitting metaphor for his life as a farmer. It was a life he had managed to escape for most of his adult years.

Dolph was Rudolph Peter Gallant, born in Rustico, PEI, in 1878, and raised on the fertile red earth he now tilled in St. Georges, Kings County. In his late teens, driven by monotony and wanderlust, with only a grade three education, Dolph left the family farm. For thirty years, he travelled and worked throughout North America: panning for gold in Alaska, constructing bridges in British Columbia, and building ships for the First World War on California's Gold Coast. He was short, tenacious and self-deter-

8

mined and ultimately became a highly-skilled millwright.

In the mid-1920's, Dolph returned to PEI to assume the operation of the Gallant family farm after the death of his father. Perhaps his roots pulled then, or mortality weighed, or maybe he was simply tired of living alone and only for himself. Whatever the reasons, at fifty, he and Jeannette began raising a family together.

The Gallant farm was one hundred acres and stretched along the southern shore of Boughton Bay or Grand River as the locals call it. Dolph and Jeannette began their lives as a couple in a small whitewashed farmhouse, which originally stood at the top of a long-sloping crest, overlooking the narrow body of blue water, fringed by evergreens and accented by a red and white lighthouse in the distance.

Daily, just before dawn, Dolph stood at their kitchen window above the sink and watched as that stunning view emerged from the darkness. He was usually on his second cup of strong tea by then, and it was a ritual that had gradually changed from appreciation to resentment over the span of a few short years.

By the time Elizabeth had become part of the family, after eight of the fourteen years he and Jeannette scraped their livelihood from that land, Dolph had already fully acknowledged consciously what his life's path had tried to tell him: he would never be truly content as a farmer.

Dolph was a realist, one who suffered very little idiocy from any quarter, and that included himself. It was the depth of the Great Depression at this point and even if it weren't, following the whims of commerce around the continent was never a viable option for a man with a family. That part of his life he had willingly traded forever, for her and for them.

That fall evening, Dolph glanced across the table at the five-

9

year-old girl they had decided to take in. Elizabeth sat directly to the left of the injured party, a close-quartered shot, Dolph noted. She had hardly moved, still staring intently at the meal in front of her, though her cheeks were now two bright roses. Although Elizabeth and Peter were the same age, she was half his size. Her head barely reached above the table and, as he watched her, Dolph felt the urge to stifle a chuckle bubbling deep in his chest.

"I suggest to you, mister," he said to Peter in his pipe-graveled voice, sliding a fresh utensil in the girl's direction, "you best stop teasing the creature. Eat, there's work to do."

3
THE BROTHERS

Flying cutlery aside, Peter and Elizabeth would become fast friends, although that one early memory held tight in Elizabeth's mind. She had braced herself, expecting a rough dressing down from Dolph, something the boys had received regularly but she had warily managed to avoid until then. She waited, but it never did come.

Instead, her new family moved on, slurping and chewing, the moment already dissipated, and in the mundane details of that everyday occurrence Elizabeth glimpsed a crack in the crusty exterior of the surly old man who smelled of wood smoke and tobacco. For Elizabeth, it was her first awareness of what the others took for granted. Dolph would have her back when and where it counted, although none could have predicted just how pivotal that tacit acceptance was for Elizabeth, nor how strong it would grow to be. Here was the seed of a unique bond, a mutual connection that until that moment had existed only on Dolph's part beginning for him the day they went to get the child in Souris.

She had been scared and confused, at first, still and quiet. Dolph did fully acknowledge Jeannette's gentle hand in Elizabeth's remarkable transition. But even so, he marveled that by the start of the first fall, Elizabeth had progressed to all but abandoning Jeannette, the kitchen ditched to watch Charlie outside or to help the boys in their routine chores as best as a five-year-old could do.

Peter was the main recipient of Elizabeth's assistance, Dolph observed at a distance, the two of them vigorous competitors now for the most henhouse eggs scooped or the capture of an unfortunate boiling-pot chicken, Elizabeth's legs churning in the chase like a couple of skinny pistons.

Dolph smiled inwardly at the sight, at the spunk and grit in the undersized being, and slowly, over time and trust, Elizabeth moved close to the center of Dolph's orbit, each recognizing in the other a fundamentally familiar nature.

Eventually, as Elizabeth's and Dolph's link strengthened, it dawned on the boys that, while they were strictly assigned their duties around the farm, and no slack allowed, the runt seemed to be able to pick and choose whatever she wanted to do, whenever she wanted to do it. The sun shone right out of her arse, they thought, the old man down right soft when it came to her, although they were careful to keep that sentiment to themselves.

Besides, they came to realize, Elizabeth's special status was shaping up to be more of a convenience than a hindrance, and one they were not above exploiting. She was puny, was their assessment, but by no means a pushover. Any problems among them Elizabeth handled herself, never manipulating through Dolph, even after it became clear she could. It was a lesson reinforced in the late hours of that first Christmas Eve.

On that night, after all were snug in their beds, Peter's excitement impelled him to sneak into the small, darkened sitting room for a preview inspection of the presents placed there by Santa. Just as he was admiring the shiny new nickel inside the pink clip wallet under the tree, a sudden, piercing screech emanated from above, shattering the quiet, demanding he "Put that back right now Mister!"

12

He did, after his "shit scare" jump nearly toppled the spindly tree, and the sonic shriek had resonated throughout the entire household. Peering through a gap at the top of the attic stairs, Elizabeth had a clear view of Peter below in the act of pilfering her present. Next morning, however, Elizabeth's eyebrows arched in utter surprise at the pink wallet from Santa, with a coin inside. Dolph sputtered his tea at the angelic expression on her face.

In time, Elizabeth was also proving useful as the boys' reconnaissance agent, trying out certain requests such as asking permission to keep an impossibly thin stray or, as Dolph put it, "another goddamn mouth to feed." She could also gauge the exact level of Dolph's annoyance at any given infraction and, in some cases, diffuse it.

Over and over during those initial years, in so many small ways, Elizabeth was resolute in her mission to be the sister, to be trusted as one of them. It was a loyalty established beyond all doubt the day the boys accidentally broke her foot.

The mishap could have been far worse, had the angle of the swinging axe-head not been altered before making full contact with the top of Elizabeth's right foot. On that day, Peter had convinced Joe it was high time he had a go at chopping the head off the boiling pot hen, while Joe held it in proper position on the block. Unfortunately for Elizabeth, buzzing around the periphery as usual, Peter's initial attempt at a full-throttled swing resulted in the axe handle sliding from his grip, rolling in mid-air, and the butt coming down with a thud on the bridge of her bare foot.

Elizabeth soundlessly collapsed, close to a faint. By the time the boys hobbled her into the house, one at each armpit, the pain was excruciating, the bridge of her foot elevated at an oddly steep angle, and she felt that she was going to throw up.

All three knew Dolph was not going to be happy with such "god-damn stunned stupidity," but the minute Jeannette was able to ask what happened, Elizabeth volunteered that she had dropped the axe on her own foot, and then she burst out crying. Later, Dolph, too, pressed for details, without much success. But he let the matter drop, knowing full well she was not telling the whole truth and the boys' uncharacteristic silence a sure sign she must be covering for them.

Within a day or so, Doc Kennedy arrived from Georgetown, about twenty miles away. At that time of year, mid-summer, dry dirt roads were passable enough that he could travel throughout his huge rural route in his ten-year-old Model A Ford. Winter or early spring required a truck to pick him up at a designated point outside the village and taxi him around, a service the Walker family provided for their St. Georges neighbours without question or charge.

Winter or summer, Doc Kennedy knew there would likely be no cash rendered for his services either, but he could count on all the spuds he could eat, a supply of undersized eggs, perhaps a few fish, whatever was in season. The best-case scenario might even involve the plucked remains of the very foul that caused the trouble in the first place.

On this visit, Doc stitched and dressed the wound and splinted Elizabeth's foot. A bone was cracked, but by the feel of things, it was not too serious a fracture.

"She'll have to stay off it six weeks or so. Best get Dolph to rig up a crutch of some sort," he told Jeannette. "I'll be back round then to take the splint off and have another look, but don't you worry, little girl," he said to Elizabeth, who was in no way worried but nodded solemnly, "won't be long and you'll be good as new."

Doc Kennedy was mostly right. Elizabeth's foot did heal, and she did regain full function of it, although it would remain permanently raised in the middle with a dimpled line in the skin from left to right.

As an adult, Elizabeth often recounted that story to her children and grandchildren, and despite a few gruesome embellishments, such as how long chickens continued running around after losing their heads, the kids loved to hear it. They received that story, and all the others, in the same spirit as they were delivered: a matter-of-fact mosaic of life in a remote Maritime community, during one of the world's bleakest times in history. For Elizabeth, those days were among her most carefree.

4

THE VISITORS

Through round, wire-rimmed glasses, Dolph read *The Guardian* headline. Cripes, he thought, peering at print that seemed smaller with each passing year, goddamn Krauts.

At a few pennies per issue, Charlottetown's daily newspaper was a treat Dolph occasionally allowed himself, and although this copy was out of date by five days, it was as late breaking a news source as one could expect in St. Georges. The paper, along with other basics such as tea, flour, or animal feed, were available twice weekly via Leo Fay's peddling wagon. Prior to the Depression, Leo's wagon had been upgraded to a two ton truck. The delivery service was an extension of the only general store in the area, owned and operated by James Fay and Sons in Newport, about five miles south. Those days, payment consisted primarily of trade, or at least the promise of one.

In 1938, news from away meant anything national or international, and competed for space with concerns from across the way, meaning the other side of the Northumberland Straight but still within the Maritimes. Both, however, were soundly trumped by Island politics, or anything else that impacted PEI directly. Dolph greedily consumed it all, front page to back, everything from who died in various counties around the Island, to rumblings of discontent overseas.

This article outlined growing tensions in Europe as Germany and Italy continued annexing their neighbours, the most recent act of aggression being the military seizure of Austria by Germany. Predictions of another world war loomed. Dolph silently thanked God their Joe was too young to be caught up in the coming fray and hoped this time the bastards would be creamed proper, and in much shorter order than the last four-year fiasco.

He continued reading at the kitchen table, Jeannette anxiously fussing about behind him, both still in their Sunday Mass clothes. Earlier in the week Leo Fay's deliveries included a relayed phone message from Jeannette's sister, Genevieve, in Souris, notifying them that Christina and Frank McIntosh were coming to see them that Sunday afternoon.

Dolph thought it unusual the couple would be travelling down by car over atrocious early spring roads, and said as much to Leo, perhaps a little more testily than he had intended, but, frankly, the prospect of their visit more than irritated him. During the two years Elizabeth had been with them, she had said very little about her old home, at least not to Jeannette or Dolph, and, the couple agreed, it was best to let sleeping dogs lie. As far as they could tell, Elizabeth had no memory of that life. The very point, Dolph thought. Obviously, everything was going along fine, so why in hell would those people feel the need to traipse down here now?

They decided not to go into details about the impending visitors, simply telling the kids company was expected from Souris that afternoon, friends of Aunt Gen, and they could leave their Sundays on, taking care not to get them dirty. Not an especially appreciated offer for the boys, but Elizabeth loved to preen about in her one plain grey jumper over a white blouse and knitted leggings. She was in the midst of thinking the outfit was somewhat diminished by the knotted red sweater and the galoshes required for their still springy yard, when the rounded contours of a black automobile took shape in the distance. By the time the car bounced to a stop at the farm house, the boys too had noticed its arrival, and all three stood shyly by as the passengers emerged. Then, like a wallop, Elizabeth saw and recognized Christina McIntosh.

5

NO GOING BACK

As an adult, Elizabeth had no memory of anyone other than Christina McIntosh arriving that day, not Frank, Christina's husband, nor their daughter, Teresa. Instead, from the moment Elizabeth laid eyes on the lighthouse lady, and with the intensity of a lighthouse beam, her mind fused on what Christina looked like, the words she spoke, and, above all, the pall of emotion and questions that lingered in her wake.

Teresa, nearly ten years old by then, remembered the day and the mood differently years later. "Dad had actually borrowed a car for us all to go down there, that day. Mum wanted to check on how Lizzie was doing, see if she liked it there."

It was a clear, sunny day, and the girls played around outside, the farm a fascinating novelty for Teresa. Lizzie had changed some and the Gallants didn't even call her "Lizzie" anymore, only Elizabeth. She had grown, Teresa noted, though she was still undersized for her age, and seemed quieter.

Eventually, Christina came out of the farmhouse to visit with Elizabeth alone. She wore a full-length wool coat with oversize brown buttons, warm for that day, but stylish, and she had on sturdy, laced shoes with thick square heels. Elizabeth hoped Christina didn't accidentally step in horse manure. They were standing at the entrance of the barn when Christina leaned over at the waist, bringing her face closer to Elizabeth's, and asked outright if

19

Elizabeth would like to go with them to see her real mother.

At that moment, Elizabeth realized she did not remember what her real mother looked like, though she did know deeply that she had one. She had always known it.

Christina went on to say that Elizabeth's real mother was engaged to be married, and if Elizabeth wanted to, she could go live with her real mother in her new house in Souris.

"G'way," Elizabeth said, amazed.

"Would you like that, Lizzie?"

"Yeh, for sure," said Elizabeth, and took off like a shot toward the house to announce the news, stopping short at the step as she heard Dolph's deep, stern voice from inside.

"Hey," she said turning to Christina behind her, "Mum and Dad can come too, right?"

Christina didn't answer, but followed Elizabeth and stood just inside the kitchen door, where there was now utter silence and Dolph's face was fire red.

"Mum," Elizabeth said, instinctively avoiding Dolph, "we can go to see my real mother, if we want, in her new house. Eh? Do you want to, Mum? Dad can come too," she added, tentatively.

Dolph pushed himself from the table, the chair scraping along the floor as he stood facing Christina. Finally, in a low and even voice, he said, "Mum and me are not going anywhere, Elizabeth. Neither are you. Go get your friend. They're leaving."

Teresa peeked over the deep rear window as the McIntoshes' car thumped its way back down the lane to the main road. Elizabeth stood in the yard watching them go and wondered why her real mother didn't come, too.

6

QUESTIONS

Elizabeth was, by then, old enough to remember the emotional jolt she felt that day, although she was in no way ready then to reconcile the confusion, the anxiety, and, irrationally, the guilt created within her by the McIntosh visit. Elizabeth was shaken by the realization that the memory of her real mother's face was nowhere to be found in her mind.

Elizabeth struggled with Dolph and Jeannette's reaction too. Generally, Dad had no trouble announcing the exact reason he was pissed off. But on that day, while he was certainly angry, she did not know why. Was he mad at her for wanting to go see her real mother? The boys were also confused by the unusual tone the day had taken, Mum curiously subdued after what would normally have been a welcomed opportunity to socialize.

In the following weeks and months, Elizabeth found herself in a quandary. How could she avoid getting her parents upset while, at the same time, dig around for answers about her real mother? Of course, she knew Mum was really the only safe source, and so Elizabeth embarked on a delicate dance. She re-attached herself to Jeannette, hanging about in the kitchen and around the house, doing all she could for Mum and, now, not one but two younger brothers. Jeannette had given birth the previous year, March 1936, to another boy, Gerald.

Eventually, Elizabeth decided to test the waters with a question she already knew the answer to. Why did the Gallants come to get her?

"We had no girls. We wanted you to be our girl," said Jeannette, confidently falling back on the original narrative. Normally, that would be followed by Jeannette telling her how far they travelled, how they got the room ready just for her, and how excited the boys were that she was coming.

That last point Elizabeth doubted, and this time, Elizabeth couldn't help herself. Now that she had gotten started, she sailed ahead. How could it be that her real mother was not married, but she already was a real mother? How did Mum and Dad know she could be their girl? Why didn't her real mother want to keep her so the Gallants would have to pick one of the other girls? Why didn't her real mother come, too, with the McIntoshes that day?

Those were the questions Elizabeth wanted to ask, but never got any further than the first one. Jeannette was absolutely not ready to answer that and Elizabeth quickly backed off at Jeannette's rare lapse into a perturbed fluster, immediately assuming a nonchalant air, unwilling to risk the push. What exactly had been in jeopardy Elizabeth could not say in words then, only that a fundamental insecurity had cautioned her, and that it simmered under the surface until three years later when Jeannette and Dolph had their sixth child—a girl.

Elizabeth was ten years old when Lauretta Margaret (Laura) was born in 1940, and even after five years of Elizabeth's life with the Gallants, she worried that her bond, her very purpose for being among them, might be threatened by the arrival of the red-faced female in a bundle of blankets. Mum and Dad had their own girl now, and Elizabeth's insecurities bubbled over completely.

22

For months after Laura's birth, Elizabeth was on hyper alert, anxiously looking and waiting for any and all signs that her place might have been usurped. But despite her diligence, Elizabeth could not discern so much as a hint. In fact, Laura's birth ultimately solidified the exact opposite. Elizabeth's connection to Mum tightened as Jeannette further relied on big sister services, her brothers seemed blissfully unconcerned with the new addition, and, most important, Elizabeth remained the apple of Dolph's eye, come what may, including Laura and then Winston, born in 1942, the official baby of the Gallant siblings.

7

LEAVING PEI

With Germany's official surrender to the Allies on May 7, 1945, one of the longest unbroken war battles in recorded history ended. The Battle of the Atlantic was a Second World War fight for the heart of the North Atlantic sea. It raged for five straight years and, by proximity and disposition, Atlantic Canadians were crucial to a brutal and costly victory.

The mission was to carry troops, ammunition, fuel, trucks, food, medicine, and other equipment and sustenance from Eastern Canada, through the German U-boat infested waters of the Atlantic Ocean to the insatiable shores of Western Europe. By 1941, the situation had become desperate. Government conscripted cargo ships were too few, and the convoys had suffered too many losses to adequately meet the need for supplies, despite substantial Allied navy and air force protection. The only solution was to build more boats, quickly, securely, and in numbers that assured the mission's success. Between 1942 and 1945, hundreds of cargo convoys launched off the eastern coast of Canada. It was this world war necessity that gave birth to the Canadian Merchant Navy.

It was also the momentum that drove an economic boom in the tiny town of Pictou, Nova Scotia, and caused, for the second time in Elizabeth's twelve years, a dramatic and fundamental change in the direction of her life.

During the first few years of the war, even as enemy subs lurked as far into Canadian waters as the Gulf of St. Lawrence, and as Europe exploded in flames and North America in frenzied production, the ebb and flow of life on the farm in St. Georges, PEI, carried on, the war hardly registering a bleep in the daily lives of the Gallants.

In the early weeks of 1942, however, Elizabeth and her brothers noticed a distinct improvement in their father's manner and mood. He was lighter, somehow, Elizabeth thought, a word rarely if ever applied to old Dolphie Gallant, and at the end of that January the mystery was solved in the form of a family announcement. There were actually two pronouncements at that winter supper table inside the wood-warmed kitchen. The first was that another new brother or sister was on the way. Jeannette at forty years old and Dolph at sixty-four were expecting the last of their seven children in early August.

Elizabeth and the boys were mildly surprised at the announcement of the new baby, Elizabeth actually wondering where in cripes everyone was going to squeeze. Laura, not yet two, was still sleeping in her parents' room, and the four boys were already crammed together every night. Possible long-term sleeping rearrangements were rumbling around her head when the second part of the news dropped like a bomb.

This new baby would not be born here in St. Georges, Mum and Dad were telling them, because by the time he or she arrived they would all be living in Pictou, Nova Scotia. The family was moving, sometime after the end of that school year but before the arrival of their newest sibling in August. They were leaving the farm, leaving Prince Edward Island.

After a minute of stunned silence, pandemonium erupted, the boys beside themselves with riotous, bouncing whoops. Dolph

25

allowed them their moment, encouraged it even. Although Pictou was a mere forty-five kilometres away as the crow flies, he knew that for his Island-cocooned brood, it was the other side of the moon. He remembered the feeling and shared it still.

History was repeating itself, both on the world stage and for Dolph, and he had jumped at the opportunity to complete his working life fully engaged, again building ships for a world war effort. It would not be on Prince Edward Island, but it would be close, just across the Strait, and this time his family would be with him.

Many of the details were lost on Elizabeth, initially. Dolph had been recruited and accepted a job with Parks Steamship Company Ltd. as a charge hand millwright to help build three cargo ships for the war effort at the Ferguson Shipyard in Pictou. He would mostly be working on the ships' launch ways and slips.

The family would eventually come back to the Island, but they would live in Pictou till the end of the war, or whenever the three ships were all safely sailed, whatever came first. They would be living in a brand new house, one of the "Victory Heights" prefabricated homes being built just for shipyard workers and their families. Next fall the children would go to the new Victory Heights School in Pictou and the new baby would be born in a modern hospital, the Sutherland Memorial. Elizabeth, however, was having a hard time getting beyond the fact that Dad would be leaving first without them.

The company required him to be in Pictou as soon as possible and his trip, in the middle of winter, would be a long ordeal: a day to reach the ferry at Borden, then another to get across the Strait to Cape Tormentine, New Brunswick, and back down to Pictou by train. In early summer, though, as soon as the ice had fully cleared,

26

the smaller, brand-new seasonal ferry between Wood Island and Caribou, NS, would take them and all their belongings to Pictou in half that time.

Everything was planned and arranged in a whirlwind, and within weeks Elizabeth stood inside the front door of the farmhouse among Dolph's packed bags, too cold to wait outside for his drive to the train station. Dolph looked at her there, quiet and stiff, suddenly seeing the five-year-old from the lighthouse.

"You know I'll be back when school is done to get you all, Elizabeth," he told her in a raspy whisper. "You know that, eh?" She nodded. "And you'll all do your bit to help Mum get everything ready?" he said louder now that the rest had assembled. She nodded again. Dolph thumbed her head and squeezed her chin. Walker Sr. honked his arrival, they said their goodbyes, and Elizabeth climbed the stairs to her room in the attic.

The family did make it to Pictou that summer, but it was late, not until the end of August, close to the start of the next school year. The cascading series of delays had been triggered after Winston Franklin Gallant made his world debut a month earlier than expected, on July 6, born not as planned in the shiny, sterile conditions of a modern maternity hospital in Nova Scotia, but like the others, in their farmhouse attended by St. Georges' midwife, Mary-Catherine Christian. The last of the Gallants had attained official Islander status, just in the nick of time.

In addition, Dolph, with most everyone else involved, had significantly underestimated the speed and urgency required for the building of the new ships in Pictou. By the time Jeannette had sufficiently recouped after giving birth and the baby had grown to a healthy weight, their allotted house had been given to another shipyard worker's waiting family. Jeannette and the kids were re-listed for the next round of fully assembled homes. By then, the first ship, the SS *Victoria Park*, was near launching and Dolph could not be spared to help with the move, not even for a couple of days.

And so, for the final time in their collective lives, the Gallants relied, again, on the quiet generosity of their St. Georges community. Leo Fay and his two-ton delivery wagon took the family to Wood Island, across the strait on the Prince Nova Ferry to Caribou, and then to Pictou. Mary-Catherine volunteered to go along, her responsibility for Winston's safe delivery extending to his new home on the mainland.

That day, the adults squeezed into the cab of the truck with the two youngest, Elizabeth and the boys in the back piled on top of and in between mattresses, furniture, pots and pans, jolted by every pothole and holding on at every corner along the way.

"We rolled into Pictou like the Beverly Hillbillies," Elizabeth recalled many years later. "The boys didn't even have shoes when we got there, had tossed them over the side of the ferry boat rail to see how far they'd bounce in the water."

Felix Walker long remembered that moving day, too. "They were supposed to come back, you know," he said, standing on the same piece of ground, in front of the same small farmhouse nearly three-quarters of a century later. "It wasn't supposed to be permanent."

The Gallants would never return to the sprawling green fields and salt-scented winds that had so thoroughly shaped them along the shores of Boughton Bay. They were saying good-bye for good that day, though they didn't know it. They were leaving not only their neighbours but a place and a time and a kind of freedom none of them would ever experience again.

28

8

THE GALLANTS IN PICTOU

It was as if the entire town had won the lottery. On October 9, 1941, the Honourable J.H. MacQuarrie made the astonishing public announcement that a small dockyard in Pictou had been awarded a multi-million-dollar contract for the construction of three 47,000-ton steel cargo ships. The town had been chosen over the much larger, better equipped, and more politically connected port of Halifax. It had been an unlikely coup and politicians at every level took the opportunity to bask in the glow of credit: some worthy, some not so much, but all hailing their hand in Pictou's return to her shipbuilding glory days.

Less often touted was the fact that Allan A. Ferguson Jr. had convinced a complicated conglomerate of provincial, federal, and British government entities that he and his three brothers could turn their retrofit and repair marine slip into the kind of shipyard that would support such a gargantuan undertaking. Operating under the official name of Foundation Maritime Shipbuilding Ltd., the brothers did just that in record time.

On April 8, 1942, the Park Steamship Company Ltd. was officially created by the Canadian government, and it ordered 160 cargo ships and twenty tankers during the next three years. The large majority of cargo ships were Park-class, named after Canada's local and national parks. They could carry ten thousand tons of cargo, the equivalent of food for 225,000 people for a week. Twenty-four

Park ships, of a modified Scandinavian-class design, were built at the Ferguson Yard in Pictou.

"The Birthplace of New Scotland," Pictou's original claim to fame, was back on the map.

None of that, however, was of much interest to Elizabeth or her siblings as they moved into their new Victory Heights rental on Cedar Street. Nor was any of the desperate scrambling by Pictou's municipal officials trying to keep up with the bursting infrastructure needs of a town that had nearly tripled its population practically overnight.

Elizabeth's main concern was the fact that she would be spending her school days apart from her brothers for the first time, no longer with them among the fifteen or so kids, grades one to twelve, in their old, one-room country school house on the Island. Within weeks of their arrival Elizabeth was enrolled in a class of about twenty at the Stella Maris Catholic Convent School, for girls after grade five, a few of them boarders, but most of them day students up to and including grade eight.

Elizabeth adapted well to the convent school. She was a good student, both in her academics, and, perhaps more importantly, in her ability to adjust to the expectations of the infamous teaching order of nuns, the Stella Maris Sisters from the Nova Scotian chapter of the Sisters of the Congregation of Notre Dame. As far as Elizabeth was concerned, the Sisters' notorious reputation was a bit overblown, despite their tendency to glide between rows of dented desks, faces pinched by stiff white cornetts, and a yardstick perpetually ready to dart from the depths of flowing black robes. The Stella Maris Sisters, Elizabeth felt, were simply maintaining their part of an agreement. If students paid attention, didn't speak out

30

of turn, and behaved respectfully, they wouldn't get smacked, and may learn something in the bargain.

All this seemed perfectly reasonable to Elizabeth, and her initial separation anxieties soon dissipated. But she did have to work on one issue early on, which was to respond promptly to her first given name, Mary. It was a bit of a mystery, not that the nuns refused to call her Elizabeth, but the power their will had beyond the walls of the convent school. Because of the Sisters of the Stella Maris, Elizabeth became Mary to her school mates, her friends, the town at large, and ultimately even to her family, and for the rest of her days she would be called Mary by everyone, with one exception. For Dolph she would always be Elizabeth.

The boys had adjustments to grapple with, too. At fourteen, Joe was in grade eight, and whether or not he completed that level, he had reached the age where many young teenagers began to make their own way, especially given the ample job opportunities that existed in Pictou at the time. Almost immediately, he was hired full-time as a general labourer in the sheet metal area of the shipyard. Joe's life as an adult had officially begun in Pictou.

The other three school-age Gallants were experiencing their version of culture shock. Unlike Elizabeth, they had never before been required to interact on a daily basis with people they had not known their entire lives. In Pictou the classrooms were huge, the teachers barely knew their names, and order was much more strictly maintained. Peter especially seemed to chafe at the impersonal and regimented nature of the large Dawson and then Victory Heights Elementary schools.

"Mister Gallant," his teacher had demanded, early on, as Peter stood in the boys' line after recess, "have you been smoking?"

Peter and his new pal, young Freddie LeBlanc, had indeed been puffing in the woods during recess, but, Peter decided, it was best to tell the woman what she would like to hear. "Nope," he answered.

With a flick of her wrist, the small pouch of tobacco and rolling papers sailed in an arch from Peter's front shirt pocket, landing with a plop on the ground in front of her heavy black shoes. His package of "makins" were then promptly confiscated and things slid steadily downhill from there.

Peter's school attendance became more and more sporadic. He and Freddie, emboldened by each other's company, skipped school every fair-weather chance they got, their days filled, instead, with explorations of a town growing and transforming before their very eyes. The pair watched and smoked as excavators dug and bulldozers rolled, as poles were sunk and lines strung, as new pipes were buried and new roads paved, all to the ringing song of iron and steel echoing from the now largely flattened Battery Hill, down at the new and improved Ferguson Yard. School could not compete.

9

FREDDIE LEBLANC

Freddie (Louis Frederick) LeBlanc was a native Pictonian, a few months older than his new school chum, Peter Gallant. He was born New Year's Eve, 1929, the sixth of John Thomas and Johanna (White) LeBlanc's eight children. Freddie's parents were both French, although they rarely spoke the language and certainly never considered passing it on to their children. For John-Tom and Johanna, anglophone assimilation had long been the best path toward making one's way, and there was no reason to believe that was going to change any time soon.

John-Tom was five feet, nine inches tall with a stocky build, a ruddy, weathered face, and a prominent nose. Prior to the war, he worked as a slip carpenter at the old Ferguson Shipyard, building the wooden cradles that held the boats for retrofit or repair. He also doubled as the shipyard diver, securing the holding blocks the ships' keels rested on prior to dry dock, the enormous steel helmet of the diving suit attached to an air hose strung from above like a giant umbilical cord.

John-Tom LeBlanc was a jovial, good-natured man by all accounts, a practiced jokester and skilled teller of tall tales. In later years, his grandchildren remembered scrambling to sit beside him at supper or anywhere else that placed them in close enough proximity for an affectionate nose tweak or ear tug.

In 1943, however, John-Tom was neither entertaining friends or teasing grandchildren. He was deep in the dangerous business of escorting cargo freighters between the western and eastern shores of the North Atlantic aboard a Royal Canadian Navy corvette anti-submarine ship. Like many of his Maritimes seamates, he had been recruited specifically to the Navy because of his experience as a sailor, increasingly in short supply as the Battle of the Atlantic raged on. Other than the rare dock into the port of Halifax and a quick day or two leave in Pictou, John-Tom was at sea for most of the Second World War while Johanna was at home raising their children alone.

Johanna was one of many wives and mothers struggling under that war-time strain, but she was an efficient manager of her household. She was short and stocky, barely five feet tall, born and raised along St. George's Bay on the rocky southwestern coast of Newfoundland. Johanna didn't talk much about her personal history or her people in Newfoundland. She and John-Tom probably met in Pictou when she came to the mainland looking for work around the beginning of the First World War. The LeBlanc children were aware of their relatives in Newfoundland, however, and Johanna did return to them once in a desperate attempt to save the life of their second eldest child, Beatrice. A colder, drier climate might help, the doctors had advised the couple, but at age seven, Beatrice died from complications of pneumococcal meningitis and was buried in Newfoundland.

It would not be until many decades after Johanna's death that her children and grandchildren would come to discover the complexity of their grandmother's Newfoundland heritage. Johanna's family were French speaking, with an English surname, but had originally descended from neither one of those European ances-

34

tries. They were actually Qalipu Mi'kmaq, one of two groups of Mi'kmaq on the island of Newfoundland who stubbornly managed to retain their original culture and identity. The Qalipu's gained official status in 2011, granted to Qalipu people who still lived in Newfoundland and/or maintained strong current connections to the area and culture.

Although Johanna's Indigenous lineage is well-documented, none of it had ever been mentioned by, nor was of any concern to Johanna. She had made a life far from St. George's long before Newfoundland was part of Canada and returned to it that one time only, with her daughter. Beatrice remains there today, under a simple stone marker on the original lands.

Regarding the couples' remaining seven children and the forty-two grandchildren they would eventually have in Pictou, Johanna was intensely connected. She did whatever was necessary or asked by any of them, at any time, perhaps not without comment, but absolutely without reservation.

Like her husband, Johanna had a flare for telling a story, with an added dash of Newfinese. But she had less patience than her husband and a tendency to speak her mind, a combination that could, on occasion, turn sharp wit to stinging barb. Young Freddie was very much like her.

Peter Gallant's and Freddie's easy friendship may have seemed an improbable alliance, at first glance. Peter had grown into an attractive lad with a quick smile and his mother's bright blue eyes. He had also inherited and honed her easy-going, effortless charm, especially effective with the ladies, he soon learned, with whom he was already enthralled.

Freddie was also a handsome boy, with a dark complexion, coal black hair, and hazel eyes; but, unlike Peter, no amount of good looks could override his unfortunate habit of saying out loud exactly what he thought, the moment he thought it. Freddie's status among sensitive teenage girls was, for the most part, the tolerated sidekick of the roguishly popular Peter Gallant.

Freddie claimed he didn't give a rat's ass what the girls thought, and for all their differences, Peter's and Freddie's friendship endured based on the one quality they did share: their innately turbulent natures, more commonly described in Pictou as "a coupl'a hellions."

Mary, as everyone but Dolph now called her, saw no reason why she couldn't continue to hang around with Peter, especially since there was so much more to do in their new town. Peter, however, balked at his little sister traipsing about with him and his buddy, even though she was the same age as they-were, and, in fact, a full grade ahead-of them. In the end Peter agreed—or more accurately Dolph decreed—that she could go to the movie theatre with him and Freddie as long as she sat in the row behind them, her presence decidedly counter-productive to Peter's goal of amassing as many girlfriends as humanly possible.

"Fine," she said, and from that vantage point Mary first got to know Freddie LeBlanc, who made her laugh right from the start, sometimes intentionally.

10

"THE HELLIONS"

Pictou's Victory Heights was a community within a community, made up of small one- or two-story pre-fabricated houses built in New Glasgow, hauled to Pictou in pieces, and assembled in a flurry on site. They were all the same, set close together on row after row of narrow streets named for various kinds of trees. It was a noisy neighbourhood, teeming with kids of all ages.

One late fall evening in 1943, just after supper, a police officer knocked on the door of Johanna LeBlanc's Heights home on Pine Street. After confirmation that he was speaking to the legal guardian of the minor youth, Frederick LeBlanc, the officer coldly presented her with a summons for Freddie's appearance in district juvenile court. The charge, he informed Johanna, was based on reliable identification of two perpetrators who had committed deliberate acts of public property destruction. A large and very expensive stack of clay piping had been cracked and punctured by Freddie and another boy. The piping, intended for the town's huge water and sewage expansion, was almost completely destroyed. In addition, the officer continued in a legalistic monotone, the youths were clearly truant from school at the time and had been reported to be habitually so.

Johanna was at her wits' end. Despite her best efforts, Freddie was maddeningly resistant to any kind of corralling, and now this. The family could not possibly afford to pay for such damage.

37

Worry burned at the pit of Johanna's stomach, with the spectre of chronic juvenile delinquency and of Freddie spiraling into a life of crime and imprisonment.

Meantime, a similar scene was taking place in the Gallant household, except that Peter was waiting for the real boom to fall, which would happen the minute his father got home from a gruelling shift at the shipyard. Peter's fears were in no way alleviated when Dolph took the news with uncharacteristic quiet, and instructed Peter to immediately escort him to Freddie's house.

There, Johanna and Dolph made their mutual introductions, and, as the two boys shuffled sheepishly around in the living room, the adults conferred in low, serious voices over tea in the kitchen. In the end, Johanna agreed with Mr. Gallant's plan, and was relieved he had the confidence to carry it out. He proposed that she allow him to appear in court on behalf of both "Christers."

Within days of his visit to the LeBlancs, Dolph stood in front of the Pictou youth magistrate to present his arguments. He began with a formal apology for any part either boy had in the destruction of the pipes, but respectfully pointed out common knowledge that the pile of piping was a favourite gathering point for most youngsters in the area. There was no real evidence, he argued, to support the claim that it was these two in particular who had destroyed the entire stock, which, he noted, had been left to open access by town officials. Therefore, he concluded, neither should be held financially, or otherwise, responsible.

As for the skipping school problem, he implored the court's understanding of special circumstances, Freddie's father being away at sea, along with his own long work hours, both by necessity of the crucial and ongoing war effort. Even so, that situation, he personally assured the judge, would also no longer be a problem.

38

The court agreed. The boys were pronounced not liable for the destruction of the pipes, and the judge accepted Dolph's word that there would be no more truancy.

It would not be the last time old Dolph intervened on Freddie's behalf, although never again in a legal setting, nor with quite the same success.

11

"GROWING UP"

Shortly after their brief brush with the law, Peter and Freddie's school problems were resolved for good, just as Dolph had pledged. They both quit entirely. By age thirteen, whatever academics the two had managed to absorb to that point would have to do. Real life lessons were waiting and they were anxious to get at it, starting with various low wage jobs in and around town, including kitchen help, coal hauling, and off and on labour at the Trenton Car Works.

"We did a stint of potato picking on the Island one time too," Fred said, remembering his and Peter's early teenage years. "Two dollars a day plus room and board for the season, a couch and salt-herring every night. Ended up hitchhiking back to the ferry with barely enough money for the boat home."

As their teenage years progressed, the boys' natural interests and inclinations began to take shape. Relatively early in his young adulthood, Peter got a job at the Bowater Mersey Paper Company, in Milton, NS, operating, repairing, and even inventing, in one instance, mill machinery. The work thoroughly satisfied him and he ultimately spent the whole of his working career there.

Freddie's transition to adulthood was different, marked by spurts and starts as he attempted to follow his inherited path and a pull to the sea. Fred loved everything about the water: playing on it, working on it, and chasing blue-grey horizons. But indulging a passion and making a living were two very different prospects.

40

Fred's first forays into the commercial fishing industry soon turned into a vicious cycle of long, hard hours for meagre profits that were largely sucked back into repair and maintenance of second-hand gear. It was a way of life for many a Maritimer, but it was not, Fred decided, for him.

More promising was a job on the historic oceanographic survey ship, the CSS *Acadia*, home docked out of Pictou. The *Acadia*, built in 1913, was considered the floating embodiment of technological wizardry for her day. She was powered by coal-fired steam engines, and Fred spent seven sailing seasons, eight months at a time, keeping those fires stoked, as the ship extensively charted the eastern Canadian coastline.

In 1976 the *Acadia* was declared a National Historic Site, an honour thoroughly warranted, not only by the fact that the ship had spent more than half a century doggedly pursuing her original mission, but because the CSS *Acadia* holds the unique distinction of being the only Canadian ship to serve in and survive two world wars. She was also the only in-port vessel to remain afloat after the blast of the Halifax Explosion in 1917.

The last year that Freddie sailed aboard the CSS *Acadia* was 1955. By that time Freddie was twenty-five years old and he had become a husband and father. The winds of post-Second World War change had arrived, and they would sweep him and his family up and carry them far.

12

MR. AND MRS. LeBLANC

Mary also experienced a few growing pains during the years that Peter and Freddie were wrestling themselves into adulthood. In 1945, Mary was fifteen years old and had finished grade eight at the Stella Maris School. The next academic step would have been high school, but, like most of the young people around her, she decided to work full-time instead, at G.J. Hamilton and Sons bakery and confectionary factory in Pictou. After a couple of years of mind-numbing factory work, though, Mary quit. Her parents were moving to Liverpool and she was going with them. From there, she tried a housekeeping job at the psychiatric hospital in Halifax, but was so traumatized by the horrific wailing of patients on her first and only night shift, she packed up and went home.

Then, at age eighteen, Mary jumped at an opportunity that came to her through friends of friends of the Gallants. She was hired to be a live-in nanny in Boston. The excitement of being on her own in a huge city in a different country was beyond words. Unfortunately, within months she was back home. The couple she worked for, she said, had her deported. Apparently, after they became aware that her legal name, Whitty, was not the name they knew her or her family by, they accused her of trying to pull a scam to get into the US fraudulently.

Mary returned to her mum and dad, who also eventually returned to Pictou for another short period. She was now nearing

42

twenty years old, and any signs of a barefoot, knobby kneed farm girl were long gone. For years, during the Gallants' coming and going between Pictou and Liverpool, Mary and Freddie occasionally bumped into each other within a larger circle of common friends. At one time, Mary's best friend, Freda Wood, dated Mary's brother Peter, which further increased Mary's and Fred's social contact. Still, although they were very comfortable in each other's company, their relationship had never been anything more than casual friends.

That all changed in the spring of 1950. Freddie had just begun a self-imposed break from his job aboard the *Acadia*. A particularly wild shore pass in St. John's, Newfoundland, had ended badly. Fred and another sailor, still under the mind-bending effects of a Screech-fueled leave, had impulsively resigned their posts aboard the ship, including a demand for immediate payout of their final wages. Eventually, the two sailors sobered up, but not before the Acadia had left without them, the remnants of their cash regretfully required to get themselves off The Rock and home to Pictou, jobless.

It was a pivotal event for Fred. Although he had few options other than to return to the drudgery of the Trenton Car Works, being home once again put him and Mary in the same social sphere. This time, though, Fred was struck by the fact that Mary was actually a full-grown woman. Suddenly, he saw her not as his best friend's kid sister, but as a friend in her own right, and a pretty one at that. Perhaps, he suggested, they should take in a show. She agreed.

Mary was not quite certain if Fred realized it, but she knew this was different. They had been to the movies lots of times together, but only as part of a larger group. On this occasion, Mary spent

43

half the day with her head wrapped in a cloth, tied in a knot at the top of her forehead, securing metal curlers that swept her fine and straight dark hair away from her face in high rolls. She wore a fitted white blouse, pinched at the waist, over a flared, red-patterned skirt, the shade matching perfectly applied lipstick, the seams along the back of her sheer stockings checked for arrow straightness before she appeared at the door, ready.

"The head on ya," Freddie chuckled after a second, in typical Freddie fashion. It was the opening line to the official start of sixty-six years as a couple. That summer, their easy friendship morphed into an intense romance, they fell thoroughly in love, and within a year, in June 1951, Mary and Fred were married.

By then, six years had passed since the last Second World War steel freighter, the SS *Lorne Park*, had been cut from her slip, plunged into the Northumberland Strait, and steamed her way toward a war-torn and exhausted Europe. The darkness had lifted at last, soldiers had come home, conscripted goods were again abundant and flowing. Like an intense burst of spring after a deep and endless winter, the world, and Pictou, surged.

The Gallants' original plan to return to PEI after the war never materialized. Well into his seventies, Dolph had instead opted for work on Nova Scotia's picturesque south-eastern shore. For a time, his unique expertise in the art of managing difficult launchings continued to pull him, and his family, back and forth between Liverpool and Pictou. In the end, it was Liverpool where he and Jeannette ultimately settled and would live out the rest of their days. The farm in St. Georges was eventually sold.

At the time of Mary's and Fred's marriage, the Gallants were completing their last stint in Pictou. The young couple were married at the Stella Maris Catholic Church, attended by a small gathering of about twenty people, family and a few friends. Fred's youngest sister, Irene, was Mary's bridesmaid, and, of course, her brother Peter stood as Fred's best man. Jeannette's sister made Mary's dress, white overlaid lace, below the knee with short sleeves, and a short tulle veil pinned to her dark hair. She held a spray of wild flowers and a heart-shaped silver pendant hung at her neckline. Fred wore a dark suit, wide-shouldered and loose-fitting in the style of the day, with a white boutonniere fixed to his left lapel.

After the ceremony, guests gathered at the Gallants' house for a reception with tea, coffee, sandwiches, and sweets, along with stiff swigs offered to the groom and shared by the men all around.

Fred's gift to his bride was a clutch of yellow baby chicks, useful he thought for a future supply of eggs or the odd stew in their newly established home. The fact that the yard of their first place on Louise Street was about the size of a postage stamp didn't occur to Fred. In any case the chicks' frequent escapes, beginning at the reception, dwindled their numbers to zero in record time. After the small party, the newlyweds boarded a bus to Prince Edward Island for a weekend honeymoon.

Deep into her old age, Mary remembered that bus ride and the anxiety she felt as it pulled away from the station heading to the ferry at Caribou. She couldn't shake the nervous energy that had taken hold that day. It had nothing to do with her choice of husband. This was the commencement of her life with Fred, and she could envision nothing that would ever make her doubt or regret that choice.

Her worry was about the life she was leaving. On her wedding day, Mary knew that the rhythm of life she had forged with Jeannette and Dolph so many years ago was officially over and

45

on that bus she felt the ties to her adopted family thinning in the stretch toward her future. It was always there on some level, the fear that those ties might not hold.

She needn't have worried. The Gallants were embedded deeply into her psyche and there they would remain in spirit and in person to the last day of her life.

13

FAMILY LIFE

The first one comes any time, but after that it takes nine months, so the old people joked, and thus, a mere five months after Mary and Fred were married, Robert Charles LeBlanc was born, November 4, 1951, weighing just over six pounds.

The intensity of new motherhood hit Mary with a stunning force: fierce, immediate, permanent. There would be other children, and in relatively quick succession for the most part, but that first shocking tide of emotion for her own flesh and blood could never be repeated. Bobby, as he was soon nicknamed, was a quick, wiry, and independent child, both in body and mind, and from his first early steps Mary was hard-pressed to contain him inside four walls.

The new family plugged along reasonably well that first year-and-a-half in Pictou, although money and space were tight, and soon to get tighter with the arrival of a second child due the end of the summer.

Nearly a decade after the war boom, Pictou's economy had slowed and employment at the Trenton Car Works was no longer as reliable. Layoffs and recalls fluctuated with the sputtering ups and downs of the peace-time market. But Fred stuck with it, had little other choice really until in early 1953 the CSS *Acadia's* 2nd Chief Engineering Officer, Paul Lavois, appeared at his door.

In years past aboard the *Acadia,* Fred and his old boss's working relationship had never risen above the level of prickly at best, and during Fred's unceremonious departure in Newfoundland things had sunk to open hostility. Yet there Lavois was, hat in hand, offering Fred his old job, over tea in the LeBlanc's cramped kitchen. Lavois explained that the *Acadia* was in dire need of an experienced sailor and a trained, coal-fired steam-engine fireman, the combination a scarce commodity.

Lavois' pitch included the more reliable employment the *Acadia* could offer, compared to the car works, along with better pay. In addition, said Lavois, falling back to his usual superior tone, now that Fred was married and settled, he was confident there would be no repeat of previous "ship and shore shit shows."

Lavois might have saved his breath. There probably wasn't much question as to whether or not Fred was going to take the job, although he did give Mary the courtesy, and Lavois the smallest of slights, by discussing the offer with her before accepting.

Mary wasn't thrilled with the idea of Fred being away at sea for long periods, but the job could allow them that bigger place in the Heights, as well as an ease up on the penny-pinching grind. She could handle things at home, and besides, she knew Fred would be far more content on the ship.

While Fred was happily up to his elbows in coal, and the *Acadia* puffed her way around jagged eastern coasts, Mary Lee Francis was born on August 24, 1953. Lee was a big baby, nearly two pounds heavier than her brother at birth. Perhaps, Mary thought, that was the reason for a much longer recoup after this second delivery, and she did have another child to chase around. But by the time Mary and Fred's third baby, Jacqueline Marie, was born in October 1955, Mary was seeing motherhood as a complete revelation. Despite all

48

the practice she'd had growing up, the twenty-four-seven work and responsibility of her own children were utterly exhausting. She was bone weary and becoming increasingly disheartened.

Dolph, too, recognized a change in his girl. He had returned to Pictou from Liverpool to help with another stubborn launching, and was staying with Mary and the kids.

"Cripes Almighty, Elizabeth," he growled after arriving at the house on Oak St., "you look like a Jesus coat rack."

Normally, Mary had no trouble seeing through Dolph's brand of gruff concern, but this time she didn't appreciate the comparison. She was defensive, unsure and critical of herself. After all, Jeannette had had more than half a dozen kids, like stair steps, and hardly missed a beat. It was what Mary thought Dolph would expect of her; it was what she expected of herself.

Dolph plied Mary with a nightly dose of black stout in an effort to "put a bit of meat on those bones." Beer, however, regardless of the potency, was not going to fix this problem. Mary was struggling and she knew it. She was disappointed in herself, but she did need help and the kids needed their father. Fred would have to quit the *Acadia*.

On the face of it, the idea that the military would be the answer to making a decent living and keeping the family together was a sound one. In 1956, when Fred enlisted, Canada was at peace in the world. Wherever Fred went as Private 1st Class LeBlanc of the Royal Canadian Black Watch Infantry, Mary and the kids would go, too, or so they reasoned.

Before the end of his basic training in Sussex, New Brunswick, Fred was notified that the family's first official posting would be to CFB Aldershot, in the middle of the stunningly beautiful Annapolis Valley. The base was only a few hours bus ride from Fred's family

49

in Pictou, and even less than that to the Gallants in Liverpool. It would be the perfect location for them all, and when Fred called with the news, Mary thought she could finally see a light at the end of what had been feeling like a slowly darkening tunnel.

Except, that flickering light would come as close as humanly possible to being snuffed out entirely.

14

SICKNESS

The cargo style van, high, long, and rounded in the front, rolled ominously through the streets of Pictou like a great white shark on the hunt. Eventually, the cumbersome vehicle took a wide turn off Union and came to a full stop about halfway up Oak Street. From her front-room window, Mary could see the words "Department of Public Health - Nova Scotia - Chest X-Ray Service" in stark black lettering below two small side windows.

Throughout the 1950s, roaming mobile chest x-ray units were a relatively common sight all over the Maritimes, part of an international effort to eradicate the persistent and deadly tuberculosis pandemic. For more than a century, consumption, the great white plague, or white death were names used to describe the insidious nature of a scourge that turned its victims to colourless skeletons long before their end. Two world wars had brought the disease home to North America in a serious way, but by October 1956, new vaccines, the invention of streptomycin, and strict public health policies had finally gained significant traction. The plague was not, however, over.

On Oak Street that day, Mary saw a group of her neighbours assembled near the van, and, of course, there was five-year-old Bobby checking things out for himself. Mary decided to take a break, more of a procrastination really. She had been trying to muster the energy to organize her household for their move to Aldershot.

51

Such an inexplicably daunting task it seemed at that moment. Fred was done with basic training and was already working there, staying in barracks while he arranged a civilian rental for them all. It wouldn't be long now.

Mary joined the other mums talking and milling about along the street in a loose lineup outside the van's narrow side door. The mobile chest x-ray service was free for adults and so the kids looked on at the oddly festive activity, the grown-ups stretching and holding their arms and upper bodies this way and that to the swishing, clacking sounds of a giant camera.

It had been a delightful impromptu gathering that afternoon. Within days, however, two men in identical grey suits stood at Mary's front door, confirming her identity and identifying themselves as representatives of the Nova Scotia Department of Public Health. One of the two, Mary remembered, did most of the talking while the other fished official looking paperwork out of a leather case, handing it to the talking grey suit, who handed it over to Mary. They declined Mary's offer to come in and so she stepped onto the stoop, trying to absorb what they were saying.

The first message was that she was a gravely sick woman, literally deathly sick, though the talker didn't use those exact words. What he did say was that Mary's recent chest x-rays showed both of her lungs were in advanced stages of pulmonary tuberculosis infection and that she was to present herself to the local Public Health Office, along with the paper work he was giving her, for immediate admission into a provincially certified tuberculosis sanitorium.

"Also," the man continued, as if he was discussing the weather, "because of this positive diagnosis, the Public Health Office will require signed authorization for follow-up screening for all others in your immediate family. All standard procedure," he assured her.

"In the meantime," another flurry of papers, "the guidelines outlined here in the information packet need to be strictly followed, things like marking and using your own dishware, towels, bedding ...that kind of thing."

The good news was that all costs incurred for hospital care, medications, and related tuberculosis tests and/or screening would be completely paid for by the government.

Mary, in a daze, managed to squeak out the only question that came to her. How long? How long would she be in hospital?

The official's guess was that surgical intervention would likely be required in her case, given the extent of the disease apparent in the x-rays, normally followed by six months post-operative therapy. All of that would be reviewed in detail at the Public Health Office, along with the pre-admission work-up.

The men completed their presentation and retraced their steps down the stoop stairs. Mary whispered an automated thank-you to their backs, but time seemed to have slowed to a stop. At her kitchen table, she stared at the papers while the magnitude of what she had just been told began to seep through.

My God, she thought, this can't be happening. But it must be bad, since they wouldn't even come inside her house. She would have to go, then? Either that or what? But how could she do that, just leave them all, her children, for six months? And what about their move to Aldershot?

The next few days passed in a complete fog for Mary, as an irrational sense of intense guilt grew and gripped her. Plans and preparations for her and the kids went into overdrive, made in a whirlwind by medical staff and extended family, as if she was already not there.

In the end, it was decided, rather than farming the kids out in

53

separate directions among relatives, Fred would continue to live in and work from the military barracks in Aldershot. He would rent a larger Heights house in Pictou, still on Oak Street, where his mother and father would live with the three kids, and where he would come home to on weekends whenever he was not on course or in the field. In addition, Fred successfully managed to have health officials admit Mary into the Nova Scotia Tuberculosis Sanitorium in Kentville, walking distance from the base in Aldershot, instead of their initial plan to send her to a facility in Cape Breton.

It was the best they could do in a bad situation.

Follow-up screenings for the kids had cleared both Bobby and Lee of the disease, and Fred had recently passed all military physical and general health testing, including for tuberculosis. Twelve-month-old Jackie, however, did not. Tests revealed she had contracted tuberculosis, probably during or shortly after her birth. The baby's case was not as advanced as Mary's, and no surgery would be required, they told Fred, but she would be admitted to hospital, the specialized pediatric tuberculosis wing of the Victoria General Hospital in Halifax. She would be there for at least six months, possibly more.

Mary was already in the pre-surgical unit in Kentville when Fred gave her the news. She was stunned, and the severe guilt she had been grappling with changed in an instant to a cold, hard fear.

Within a day of her arrival at the Kentville facility, Mary was surprised when a pretty, dark-haired woman in her forties, with a thick Eastern European accent, introduced herself as the physician who would be in charge of Mary's case. Rumour was that the lady doc was a refugee from some war-torn country, Poland maybe, and that she had made her escape to Canada before the end of the Second World War.

54

Whether or not that was true, Mary didn't know for sure, and there was no point in trying to remember the doc's last name, because she could not pronounce it anyway. She did know that her first name was Anne.

"She had very dark eyes," Mary said, "that always looked tired, but they were kind eyes, and it seemed to me that she understood."

Mary never forgot the woman, not only because female doctors were rare at the time, but because of what this doctor needed to tell her that first day they met, and how she managed to say it. Mary's pre-operative bloodwork results showed that she was pregnant, probably a little over a month along. Therefore, it would not be possible to do the surgery yet because of the severe danger the general anesthetic would present for a developing fetus. The concern was not that the anesthetic might induce a miscarriage. At this early stage it probably would not, but there would be an extremely high risk of birth defects.

Unfortunately, going home for the duration of the pregnancy and coming back after the baby was born was not an option. The Department of Public Health would never allow it, nor would it be the best thing for Mary. Instead, they would treat Mary for the tuberculosis for the next eight months in the hospital with rest and antibiotics. That should keep the progress of the disease at bay, at little or no risk to the baby. They would proceed with the surgery after she had recouped from the delivery.

Mary stared at the doctor as the woman tried her best to soften the blow, to reassure her patient that she and all the medical staff would be with her every step of the way, and that the plan was to get her home in as short a time as possible, maybe as soon as eighteen months if all went well.

Mary listened politely and nodded her head in agreement, but by the time the doctor left Mary recognized clearly where things stood. It was really no longer about when she would go home; the question was now if she went home. And the answer, she knew, was going to be up to her.

15

THE "SAND"

Mary inhaled at the sudden, deep stab in her lower back. She waited. Another followed about fifteen minutes later, then another. The familiar rhythm of labour pains had arrived at last, and although she was nervous for the baby and for herself, she welcomed the onset, glad that they were both finally moving to the next phase of the ordeal.

She had been eight months in "the Sand," the name that she and her co-patients used to refer to their hospital campus. The Kentville Tuberculosis Sanitorium consisted of the main clinical facility, a large grey building surrounded by a few smaller, more residential-looking places. In each of those, row after row of multi-paned windows resembled, from the inside, framed pictures of ever-changing seasons. The sanitorium was full to capacity with men, women, and some children from all over Nova Scotia, and a few from PEI. Mary could easily pick out the Islanders, their soft accents and clipped expressions a kind of melancholy music to her ears.

Separated by not much more than the width of their night stands, the women on Mary's ward bonded. They drew companionship, consolation, and strength from one another and were genuinely happy for those who got to go home, each success propping up their own hopeful journey. Too often, however, more than any dared talk about, she and the others were captive witnesses to the

57

last days of a life, spent in a crowded, impersonal hospital, separated from family, especially children, for the sake of those children.

"There was a wedding on our ward one time," Mary recalled, "We all got spruced up cause we were the only guests allowed. They had the ceremony right there at her bedside, with the priest and everything. The bride was in her early twenties, but she was so sick and they both knew she was never leaving that hospital. Still he wanted to marry her, he loved her that much."

Years later, Mary realized how numb she had forced herself to become, a protection against that heart-wrenching experience, and others equally tragic, in an iron determination not to be one of them. She was lucky in many ways, she preached to herself. Bobby and Lee were together and being taken care of by grandparents who loved them, and this baby coming would be too. She also had a husband close by to visit.

Every week day, if Fred was not in the field, Mary listened for those visits, her ears attuned to Fred's boot-steps coming down the corridor. Most often he arrived still in his army fatigues after supper. He would have already eaten at the base, but regularly he'd bring dessert for himself and Mary, as well as the other ladies on her ward, a bake shop pie or cookies. Mary was tickled that a few of the other patients looked forward to his arrival nearly as much as she did. Weekends were different, and Mary in no way pined for Fred to be with her then. He was with their kids, and those weekends, through him, were the only connection she had to her children.

Nighttime was when Mary most felt the strain of her situation with the sound of crying children on nearby units, or was she dreaming about her own child, in hospital, sick and crying for her mother? At times she would have to work hard to climb out of a

58

deep sink hole, and remind herself that her little girl was doing fine in Halifax. Fred could go see her on occasion and reported to Mary in minute detail everything about those visits. She was being well looked after there, he assured Mary, getting lots of attention because she was so tiny, and she would be home in no time, healthy as a trout, as Dolph liked to say.

On that late spring day, there in the Sand, Mary's labour pains intensified. Finally, in the wee hours of June 6, 1957, Mary's and Fred's fourth child, Anne Maria LeBlanc, was born, named for the lady doc with the tired eyes who delivered her.

"You know," said Isabel MacDonald many decades later, "every nurse has a case in their careers that sticks with them, for whatever reasons. For me, that case was Mary and her baby. It was not a common thing to have a pregnant patient in a tuberculin hospital. Mary was the only one we had in the five years I worked there."

In 1957, Isabel MacDonald was a young nurse, fairly new in her career, working out of the Kentville Hospital. She connected with Mary. They had a great deal in common; they were about the same age, Isabel was originally from Pictou, and, as with Mary, her husband was a military man, part of the Black Watch Regiment in Aldershot. The hospital was close for Isabel, who was assigned primarily to the operating room but worked in various capacities wherever she was needed. On the night that Anne was born, it fell to Isabel to whisk the baby away minutes after her birth to the Wolfville Hospital seven miles east.

"That was the standard procedure, I know," Isabel recalled, "but it was heartbreaking. Babies born to mothers who had TB had to be separated immediately, the moms not allowed to hold their babies for so much as a second after all they had gone through to have a healthy child."

59

On her way to the Wolfville Hospital with the infant, Isabel imagined Mary acutely distraught, a normal reaction under the circumstances. In reality, after the long, grueling labour and delivery, Mary had to will herself to stay conscious just long enough to hear that the baby was a girl and seemed healthy. Days passed before she had the strength to stay awake any more than a few hours at a time, and then she had to ask again to be sure she had heard correctly.

In Wolfville, little Anne, three days old, was officially declared free of the tuberculin bacteria and released to the care of her grandmother in Pictou.

Fred, too, was relieved that the baby was fine and the real work toward Mary coming home, to their new home with their children under one roof, in one town, could finally begin. Right now, as he presented Anne to his mum, bundled safely in an open Heinz Beans box for the trip, he felt stretched all over hell and creation, trying to keep his job straight and his family connected, fed, and happy.

There was no money for a car, certainly not one reliable enough to get him back and forth to Pictou every week, plus the odd trip to Halifax. His Private 1st Class pay barely covered the increased rent for the bigger house in Pictou, along with the upkeep of his growing brood there, never mind car payments and gas.

His brother-in-law, George, married to his oldest sister, Marion, frequently helped out with rides, but Fred couldn't ask that of him every weekend, not for that distance. There was a bus, but that cost money too and ate up most of his days off by the time it stopped at all the pick-ups and drop-offs along the way.

The only option was hitch-hiking, which he did rain or shine, even snow or shine, usually dressed in his military uniform to

60

ensure a faster pick-up. Besides, no one begrudged a soldier his warm-up or cool-down swigs of rye whiskey, or whatever else he had on hand for the trip, always graciously shared with the driver. By the time he reached Pictou, Fred was generally feeling a bit better about his family's strained situation.

The kids seemed to be managing well. Bobby had started school, and had become especially attached to his grandfather. John-Tom was by then a pensioned war vet, with lots of time and patience for the little guy, and, usually with a Currie cousin or two in tow, Grampy LeBlanc vigorously nurtured Bobby's obsession with all things outdoors.

Lee, too, had settled into the routine of life with her grandparents. Grampy was a funny, loving soul. Her grandmother was more strict, but she was always there, and Lee felt reliably dependent on her Nanny.

They also had each other, Bob and Lee, just as the grown-ups had planned. Annie, as their new baby sister was immediately nicknamed, came later and Jackie, who was also sick and in a different hospital from their mum's, had been gone from their conscious awareness for nearly ten months. By the time all four siblings were reunited, after nearly a year and a half, it was too late. Bobby's and Lee's pact was full at two, forged out of sheer instinct with the sudden, scary disappearance of their mother. It was a bumpy sibling relationship at times, but one that bonded them together, from that point on, regardless of time, space, or circumstance, and for the rest of their lives.

16

THE FIGHT

Mary was getting impatient. It was now weeks after the baby was born and still no date was set for the surgery. The lady doc had said the surgeons and the anesthesiologist wanted tip top blood work results first, whatever that meant, plus they were hoping she would gain a bit more weight.

Mary argued the point. She felt perfectly fine, and wasn't that the deal, the baby and then the surgery? Fred attempted to cheer her up with news of Jackie. The doctors in Halifax had told him that soon they would be discharging Jackie, she was doing so well, growing like a weed. That last part wasn't exactly true, but he threw that in anyway. What he didn't say was that he was not sure if the kid even knew who he was during that last visit, and that he, too, was beginning to wonder if they were ever going to wake up from this nightmare.

Finally, after a long, hot summer, the date for the surgery was set. The primary surgeon reviewed with Mary what they had already told her before the discovery of her pregnancy. They were going to do what they called a "resection" of her lower right lung, which meant removing that part of her lung altogether, thereby halting for good the progression of the disease on that side. On the smaller left lung, a pneumothorax was planned, or "collapse therapy" of the lower lobe. The idea was that the lack of oxygen to that part of the lung would kill the TB bacteria, after which the lung would eventually re-inflate itself. All that would be followed by about six months post-surgery healing and therapy.

"Great, let's go," said Mary, though she was as scared as she had ever been in her life.

Fred arrived early for a squeeze and smooch before she was rolled off toward the operating room. He left the hospital and came back a couple of times, eventually losing track of the waiting time. Other surgical patients emerged from the OR, adding to Fred's agitation, before Mary's surgeon finally appeared to tell him it was over. Everything had gone well. Fred could go see Mary in recovery, but it would be a while before she woke up.

Fred felt a flood of relief as the surgeon talked. He thanked him, followed him to the post-op area, and was directed to Mary's bedside behind a sliding tan curtain, where he was utterly unprepared for what he saw: machines beeping and blinking and poles, with lines strung and crisscrossed, crowding the cramped space. Fred found his way to the top of the narrow stretcher. There he saw tubes erupting from Mary's chest, arms, nose, and mouth as she lay in the midst of it all, so impossibly small and thin, wisps of dark hair from underneath the surgical cap the only visible contrast between her and the white sheets.

He stood by her bedside, transfixed, ashen, till he felt a light weight on his arm and realized someone was saying his name. It was Isabel MacDonald.

"Freddie," she said, getting his attention and looking straight into his eyes. "Listen to me Fred. I know how bad this must look to you right now, but it isn't. I'm telling you, Mary did very, very well. She is doing very well. She will be fine."

It was the gentle authority, the quiet confidence that Fred needed to hear, exactly when he needed to hear it, and, years later, Fred told Isabel how much her words had meant to him in that suspended moment of time.

The beginning of recovery was excruciating, inside and out, when Mary awoke enough to feel pain. Left and right incision tracks started at the top of her shoulders, traveled down to the bottom of both shoulder blades, and swooped around to the front where drainage tubes remained for several more days. Still, she was happy, the countdown to home was truly on, and her impatience to get there rose in steady proportion to her ever-increasing strength.

Fred assured her things were percolating. Jackie, now almost two, was home, healthy and hearty, though he did admit she seemed a bit bewildered as to who everyone was and strangely happy to see anyone in white, particularly the public health nurse. But she was great. They were all doing wonderfully and Fred even had a line on a car, a '47 Chev. It had a few miles on it, but was still a sweet deal.

That would be nice, Mary thought, picturing them all together out for a weekend drive, like a normal family. Once they were given Mary's discharge date, which should be soon, Fred was saying, he could secure their civilian housing in the Aldershot area. They might have to stay in Pictou a bit longer with his parents in order to avoid paying rent for the old place and the new one in the same month, plus damage deposit.

"But it'll probably be good to have them around for a while to help you out at the start anyway," Fred added.

"Oh, well, you know Fred, they'll likely want to get their own smaller place as soon as possible. They've already done so much," Mary said. "Besides, I'll be fine."

"They really do want to." Fred sounded more enthusiastic than he actually was, and Mary decided to drop the subject.

At last, in late spring 1958, nearly two years after that fateful knock on their front door, Fred loaded Mary's small bag into the back of their new-to-them Chevy. The day Mary had feared might never come had finally arrived. In her purse was the handmade autograph book she had been given by her co-patients, filled with good wishes and farewell notes from those who had most close-ly shared and understood the work, the tears and the struggles of these past twenty-two months. It was bittersweet to know she probably would not see any of them again, despite promises that they surely would.

Mary waved to the faces crowding the paned windows, as she and Fred pulled away. It was as if she had been living in a time warp, everything in her life having ceased, fighting for this day, and now it had come, and although she emerged battle scarred and bruised, she was alive and ready to reclaim her old life.

17

THE HOME COMING

Unfortunately, Mary barely recognized her old life and, worse, it barely recognized her. Annie and Jackie, nine months and two-and-a-half years old, did not know who she was and, of course, both were too little to pretend they did. What Lee understood was that her mother was coming to live at their house. She had been sick in the hospital a long time. Lee knew this because Nanny and Bobby had told her so. Her mother would be happy to see how big she was now, Nanny said. She was going to be five on her next birthday.

At seven, Bobby unequivocally remembered his mum and knew that this was a return to them as a family. He had struggled hard after she had left. Early on, frequent outbursts of temper expressed his deep-seated distress. Bobby was a headstrong child at the best of times, and during these difficult times Nanny LeBlanc never could fill the void of his mother's absence, not even temporarily. Johanna could see this, too, and worried about the same kind of swirling commotion, impulsiveness, and resistance to the slightest restraint that marked his father's nature growing up.

Whatever the kids did or did not consciously remember, it was homecoming day and Mary was determined to be festive about it, keeping to herself the fact that she really did not feel as if she had come home. They did have to return to Pictou, with her in-laws, immediately after her discharge to wait for vacancy of their new rental in the Valley. But it was not her cozy familiar house. It was on the same street, but the house Fred had secured for his parents and the kids in Pictou when she left for the hospital was bigger. Most significantly, this house had been set up, organized, and run, in every way that counted, by Johanna. That included her kids. Weeks turned into two months, and still they all continued to gravitate automatically to their grandmother.

Naturally, Mary and Fred reasoned, mostly Fred in their private moments, it was going to take a bit of time for the kids to adjust to the new order, and Fred's parents had been such a godsend in their time of need. Mary assured Fred she was just as thankful for his parents as he was, but she also felt that as long as her in-laws lived with them under the same roof, she would never be ruler of her own roost. Those were the words she used, but what she couldn't express was the fact that fully reconnecting with her children was not as easy as she had expected. The move to Aldershot could not come soon enough for her.

Finally, their new place was ready. It was in the town of Canning, situated close to the shores of Minas Basin, about fifteen kilometres from the base. The LeBlancs' rental was the bottom half of an up and down duplex, with tons of space. Unfortunately, Fred's parents assumed some of that space was meant for them, and suddenly, Fred found himself in an extremely difficult position.

Fred was fully aware that what his parents had done for him and his family during the past two years was incredible. He was especially grateful for his mother. She had taken on his three kids, four with Jackie home, all under age five, ultimately including a newborn, and all for much longer than anyone had originally expected. Johanna had been his rock. He knew there was no possible way he could have managed without her. Even with their support, things had been hard, the stress of juggling it all more than once relieved by a stiff drink. But Fred was looking forward to just him and Mary and the kids, back together, in their private abode. He longed for their old life and he knew that Mary's desire for the same thing was probably ten times stronger.

For nearly two years, however, his parents' lives had been completely invested in and intricately entwined with the kids and the family. Johanna was especially committed, as if they were her children. She had no intention of leaving them, and Fred was not about to tell her she had to. By the time the family was ensconced in their new digs in Canning, the tension between Johanna and Mary was palpable. Everything Johanna did or said was now interpreted by Mary as undermining her rightful place, and the ongoing friction was spilling over to encompass Fred's and Mary's relationship.

Mary wanted the situation resolved, but she genuinely did not want to hurt or insult Johanna either. She felt her in-laws would better understand their desire to have their new home to themselves if the request came from their son. That way, at the very minimum, they would see that she and Fred were a united front. Fred, however, seemed to prefer the path of least resistance. Rather than confront his mother and risk a serious rift between them, or put himself between the two women, or even suffer the generally strained atmosphere in the house, Fred regularly opted to hoist a few at Walter Dill's down the road, or anywhere else his drinking buddies gathered.

Around the time Fred drunkenly careened the Chevy into the town monument on Main Street, but before things had boiled over completely, a solution to his delicate domestic problems presented itself: Germany.

68

18

THE POSTING

Particularly galling for the Soviets at the end of the Second World War were the Americans. The United States had entered the war the same year as the Russians did, yet claimed the biggest say in the division of spoils. To the Soviets' way of thinking, had it not been for Russia's fierce defence of their homeland on the Eastern Front, at an estimated cost of eighteen million Soviet military and civilian fatalities, Western Europe and the Allies would never have overcome an even more concentrated Nazi war machine.

After the Soviets blockade of Berlin in 1948, America and its Western European allies responded to Stalin's post-war resurgence efforts with a vow to halt any further expansion of it, anywhere on earth. The Cold War was on.

By 1959, the geopolitical rivalry had become downright icy and Canada, part of the NATO alliance, had just increased its military presence in West Germany by three more infantry brigades and upped the posting time for the Black Watch replacement battalion to three years. At that point, including Canadian Air Force and Navy personnel, seven thousand Canadian military personnel were standing guard against Soviet Communist encroachment all over western Germany.

Freddie was determined to be among them, which required a clean bill of health for Mary, official certification that she was completely tuberculosis free, in order for her and the kids to be granted entry into Europe. He obtained it, signed, sealed, and delivered directly by the Medical Director at the Nova Scotia Tuberculosis Sanitorium. It was official, the family was moving to Germany.

Reluctantly, Fred's parents accepted the fact that their role in the daily lives of his family was coming to an end. It was a steep adjustment for them, being without the kids, especially the baby. They did suggest that perhaps Annie should stay with them while they were overseas. Inside, Mary was appalled that they would think she would even consider leaving her baby in Canada now that she was recovered. She managed a polite "no thank you," however, and the senior LeBlancs' empty space was soon filled by their large extended family back in Pictou.

In the meantime, Mary and Fred had work to do. Their furniture would have to be stored for the three years; Fred would have to sell the old Chev; they would have to organize and pack up the belongings they would take with them; medical inoculations, passports, and other records would have to be updated; and, last but by no means least, Mary and the kids would take advantage of an extended visit with the Gallants.

They stayed a month in Liverpool and Mary soaked up the precious time with her parents. She and the kids dropped in on her brothers and their families frequently, all but two of whom had married and settled in the Liverpool area. The kids played with their Liverpool cousins. Mary laughed and reminisced with her family. Occasionally, Jeannette broke into an old Island step and song, while Dolph growled, smoked, and sipped stout.

Soon it was time to go and Mary was excited and ready, but as always, leaving loosened tightly-packed anxieties. They were taking the bus back to Aldershot, since Fred had sold the car, to begin the overseas trip from there. Dolph was now eighty-one, and though

70

he was tough as a boot, she could feel his age as she gave him and then Jeannette a last hug. Three years was a long time, she worried.

She waved at them through the grimy bus glass and wondered what they were thinking. She hoped they were proud of her, as she and the kids embarked on the adventure of their lives.

19

GERMANY 1959 TO 1962

The Sergeant Major bellowed for an orderly lineup on the boarding dock, albeit less successfully than he was accustomed to, now that the area was full of not only his soldiers but also their racing kids, crying babies, and harried wives. It was spring, 1959, and the 1st Battalion Black Watch (RHR) of Canada and their families, well over a thousand people in total, had arrived by train from Halifax to Wolf Cove, a mile north of Quebec City, along the St. Lawrence Seaway. They were boarding the *Italia*, a passenger ocean liner requisitioned by NATO for the ten-day trip across the Atlantic Ocean to Rotterdam, Holland.

It was a beautiful ship and during the entire voyage Mary couldn't help but feel a tad regal. Meals were prepared by chefs and served by uniformed waiters in ornate dining halls. She and the girls, like three pampered princesses, strolled the shining, wood-railed deck or sunned on outdoor loungers, retiring to their cleaned cabin at the close of a leisurely day.

Apart from the fancy meals, Mary didn't see all that much of Fred. He and Bobby shared their own cabin, and Fred, ever the social butterfly, especially among a crowd of his peers, was enjoying himself too. Sometimes Bobby was with him, sometimes he was with his mother, but neither seemed all that concerned that the eight-year-old often explored with a swarm of other untethered army brats.

Mary might not have been quite so relaxed had she known the ship was heading straight to the scrap dock to be reduced to razor blades immediately after that crossing. And whether or not the foreign staff aboard the ocean liner appreciated such a steep departure from their usual list of entitled, well-to-do passengers is hard to say. As it was, though, she and the boisterous crowd of Canadian military families thoroughly enjoyed the *Italia's* last sail.

Soon, however, their floating vacation was over and reality in Werle, Germany, was upon them. The families arrived from Rotterdam by train and were dispersed into various living arrangements in and around the small German town. Mary and Fred opted for a married quarters apartment building, filled with other Canadian military families. It was a three-bedroom furnished apartment complete with a television set, which thoroughly thrilled the kids, despite the German-only programming.

All four kids adjusted in their own ways to the enormous change in their daily lives that began in 1959. The two oldest were enrolled in the DND school for Canadian military kids in Germany, and Jackie in kindergarten. Bobby, like his dad before him, had difficulty being cemented to a chair all day and his pent-up energies often found him in hot water in and out of school. At first, Mary tended to tip-toe around their delicate reconnection process, but she was getting frustrated with his frequent refusal to listen to her, his refusal, she couldn't help but feel at times, to recognize her as the mother of their household. In addition, he seemed perpetually mad at her.

Lee, on the other hand, did very well at school, although she and her mother were also butting heads, for different reasons. More than any of Mary's children, Lee was a carbon copy of her mother in temperament. She was fiercely willed, intensely devoted to her emotional connections, and willing to maneuver extravagantly in defence of them; and, in the beginning in Germany, Lee missed Nanny with very little sign of relenting. All understandable reactions for a young family in their unique circumstances. However, in Mary's unconscious drive to make up for the time lost and to regain her view of normalcy, she had a tendency to force the issue, and, on some subliminal level, Mary and her two oldest children continued to carry the undercurrents of anger and hurt.

Adding to what Mary believed were adjustment issues for her and the kids was Fred's ongoing celebrations since the start of their European move. Early on in their posting, after one of many suppers Fred had missed, she and all four kids appeared at what had become Fred's frequent haunt, the Red Roof Tavern.

"Mary?" Fred said, surprised and trying to cover his embarrassment in front of a full table of sloshed buddies. It was a rare sight for a woman to appear in the pub, never mind one trailed by a pack of kids. "What are you guys doing in here?"

"We're waiting for you," said Mary, steely-eyed. "As usual."

"Oh," said Fred, the pals now awkwardly staring into their beers. "Well, Mary, you don't need to do that dear," he said, trying hard to maintain a pleasant tone. "It's late. You guys go home and I'll be right there."

"No." Mary ushered the kids toward a nearby table. "We're waiting here."

"Listen Mary." Fred got up and hissed into her ear, "What the hell are you doing? Christ, it's too goddamn late for the kids to be roaming around and they shouldn't be in here anyway. Go to Jesus home."

"I said we are waiting here for you, till you decide to go to Jesus home," Mary hissed right back. "And that is what we are doing."

74

Bobby had been excited about them all getting to go the Red Roof Tavern. They hardly ever got to eat out anywhere and he was thoroughly disappointed they couldn't even stay long enough for a schnitzel. They had barely sat down when they all had to get up and go home again—his Dad included.

The incident had its intended affect and did manage to curb Fred's excessive socializing, at least for a time. But drinking was such an embedded part of military culture, then, that no one asked for or expected a full-scale stop, including Mary. That's who Fred was, after all, very similar to her brothers, hardworking and hard playing, too. That particular problem, as well as the conflicts with the two oldest kids, were nothing more than temporary post-illness realignment issues, Mary insisted to herself. Eventually that would all work out, and, in the meantime, they would make the most of their European home.

The locals in Werle were friendly, pleased with the increased business the Canadians brought. Generally, though, the community of Canadian military families did tend to flock together and Mary and Fred built friendships with them that endured for the rest of their lives.

They travelled around with those friends, each summer, as far as inexpensive day trips and their '51 VW bug could take them. They invested in a good camera and a well-made German slide projector, posed in front of historical monuments and tourist sites, picnicked along their travel routes, and wandered through bustling markets and zoos. In Germany and nearby Holland, they could feel the somber residue of a Nazi concentration camp or the genuine esteem the Dutch still held for their Canadian liberators, all in a single day.

Three years of grainy slides, each one triggering the memory of a story behind the snap, chronicled a young couple living as heartily and as fully as their circumstances allowed after the darkest of days. And for decades, that old Braun projector served as the vehicle for a visual diary, freezing the laughter and love that were there in abundance. But if one looked closely, starting with those early European scenes, and among the hundreds of photos to come, one could occasionally glimpse intrusions.

After what felt like a whirlwind three years, Fred received notification that their return to Canada would happen in April 1962. They would be heading for Camp Gagetown, a new infantry base in New Brunswick. Before that occurred, however, and with barely seven months to go, Mary had to deal with a significant loss from afar. Her gut rolled at the first words in a letter she received from her mother.

"Dear Mary, I need to tell you the news of Joe's death ..."

On September 2, 1961, her oldest brother had died in an airplane crash. Mary could not believe what she was reading. Joe, so young and vibrant, only thirty-three years old, married with two small children in British Columbia, was gone.

Immediately, the awful irony struck her. For as long as Joe had been traveling the world with the Merchant Marines, Jeanette had harboured a worry, tucked in the back of her mind, about dangerous seas and shady ports, but when he had married and settled down to raise his family in Prince Rupert, B.C., on the Pacific coast, her mind had eased. He seemed to be doing well, and had become part owner in a sheet welding business there. He had been on a hunting trip, Jeannette wrote in the letter, when the small plane he and a few friends had chartered went down into the Skeena River, deep in the rugged terrain of the northwestern interior of British Columbia.

76

Mary and Joe's relationship had never been as close as hers and Peter's, but she had so admired him. He had carried the mantle of being the oldest with such a confident maturity. Mary mourned the handsome, dark-haired boy of her childhood and grieved, too, for the loss of the uncomplicated life they had shared on that wind-swept Island farm a world away and a lifetime ago. Her heart ached, not just for her brother and his young family, but for her parents. They must be devastated and she had no real way to comfort them. She was ready to go home.

20

NOOTKA STREET, OROMOCTO

At the beginning of the Cold War, there wasn't any one place in the country big enough to handle the kind of large-scale combat training that NATO was asking of its Canadian contingent. Should the Allies need to defend western Europe beyond just standing guard, Canada would be expected to supply entire divisions of well-integrated, operationally trained, and ready to move soldiers. It was a massive commitment by Ottawa, and would require a huge swath of natural land for training, close to an established railway network, with quick access to an Atlantic all-weather seaport.

Approximately 1,100 square kilometres of mostly lumber and farm lands in southwestern New Brunswick fit the bill perfectly. The area was thirty minutes from the province's capital, Fredericton, and an hour from the Bay of Fundy seaport in Saint John.

The New Brunswick government was fairly salivating at the millions of dollars the project would bring to the province's slumped economy, hailed at the time as the biggest military training base in the British Commonwealth. The official announcement was made in 1952. The plan gave the stunned rural inhabitants of about twenty small communities and villages between Oromocto, to the north, and Welsford, to the south, one year to accept an expropriation offer they couldn't refuse and clear out. A few residents stubbornly resisted their properties being taken from them, expropriation package or not, and for years the occasional old home could be seen still standing, even as military operations were in full swing all around.

For the affected section of the Oromocto Indian Reservation, as it was known then, no compensation was offered. Instead, the federal government simply attempted to move those people, by two ton trucks, about forty kilometers up river to Kingsclear. The general idea was that they would assimilate with another group of Maliseet people there. Within short order, however, most of them had magically reappeared back on the Oromocto Reserve, tightly squeezed into their now significantly reduced ancestral grounds, whatever housing they had before already demolished.

It would take more than three decades of legal wrangling to prove the small band's treaty rights had been grossly violated, never mind their human dignity. Eventually, nearly a generation and a half later, each member of the band did receive a comparatively small lump sum of cash.

Overwhelmingly, however, New Brunswickers were happy with the deal, especially the six hundred or so original white residents of Oromocto. With military precision, the village was expanded to become the separate bedroom community for nearly fourteen thousand incoming Camp Gagetown soldiers and their families. In 1956, it was heralded as Canada's Model Town with rows and rows of various kinds of Private Married Quarters (PMQ's), along with new schools, a small shopping centre, and other supporting infrastructure, all on hundreds of newly paved streets. Many of those street names, like the name of the town itself, echoed the haunting Indigenous presence of the area and other regions of Canada.

In the spring of 1962, Fred, Mary, and the kids arrived at their new home at 4 Nootka Street, Oromocto, New Brunswick. The family's trip back to Canada aboard the faster, more modernized *Saxonia* was not quite as enchanting for Mary as her first sail across the Atlantic. Mary had prepared exhaustively for the military "march out inspection" of the PMQ apartment, but, after walls, windows, and floors were scoured to a gleaming nub, Jackie had taken a flip on the slippery shine, right onto her face, and drove her two front teeth through her upper lip. On the boat home, food had to be dropped into her swollen mouth like a nesting baby bird. Bob, at nearly eleven, was even harder to contain this trip and Lee now expected to be allowed to trail him around wherever he went.

Nonetheless, everyone was excited to be going home, although Bob's and Lee's ideas of exactly what that meant varied with their levels of foggy memories. Jackie and Annie had no memory of home. Their visions of the enigmatic Canada aligned with their mother's wistful memories: breezy summers, fields of green, lighthouses, and long, wide stretches of sandy beaches. No one, however, envisioned what they actually arrived to in April of that year: a classic New Brunswick spring blizzard.

Despite the weather, the family quickly settled into their two-story PMQ. They considered themselves lucky. Many incoming families had to secure their own civilian rentals, while on a six-month wait list for the more affordable military housing. At that time, there were so many families and kids in the town, most of the seven new schools built to accommodate them required additional mobile units to contain the overflow.

For the LeBlanc family, Nootka Street would be their neighbourhood for the next six years, a place where kids played in the streets, in the woods, on outdoor fields and natural ice, in games they

80

made up and refereed themselves. They played outside in warm summer rains or, on the coldest of days, in the highest snow forts they could create. They chased the "mosquito truck," inhaling plumes of mosquito-killing pesticides, or swarmed at the ringing bell of the "popsicle" cart, their ability to hear it from blocks away uncanny. They bought candied apples for a nickel out of one enterprising neighbour's kitchen window, and took themselves to loud and packed Saturday matinees at the Base Theatre, where twenty-five cents paid for admission, a small pop, and a bag of popcorn.

The new town was full of such neighbourhoods, one hardly distinguishable from the next. Within them, everyone knew everyone, parents and kids alike, not just on their own little road, but in their entire area. Most moms were "stay-at-home" with husbands who were absent for long periods of time, and most leaned on each other heavily.

Mary, however, was not one of them. It was simply not part of her DNA. She was always friendly, though, and maintained good relations with her neighbours, even after Bobby peppered their frozen sheets on the line full of BB gun holes. But Mary was never the drop in for tea or ask for a hand type, even though that first year in Oromocto had its challenges.

Growing, active kids naturally made for a busier household. In addition, within months of their return to Canada, Jackie contracted Hepatitis A, the virus transmitted by contaminated food or water. She was a seriously sick kid for much of her first grade, and had to repeat that year entirely.

Regardless, Mary had fully expected and was completely ready to fend for her children and rely on herself in their day to day lives, while Fred was on course, or in the field, or gone for half a year on peace-keeping tours, Cyprus being the latest one. What Mary was

81

not ready for, what she was thoroughly struggling with, was the increasing amount of time she and the kids were alone, even when Fred was home.

Fred had been back from his six-month deployment to Cyprus a little over a month by that second summer on Nootka Street. It was a Saturday morning and Mary readied her brood for a relaxing day at the beach. They called it "the beach," though in Mary's mind the narrow, pebbly shore of French Lake wasn't much of one. But the kids liked it and French Lake wasn't far from Oromocto, a ten-minute drive toward Geary, down the Waterville Road to the bend, then a right turn and a couple more bumpy miles to where Fred would park their old Studebaker in a cleared space at the bottom of a wide, low-sloping hill. At the top of the slope, off to the right, was a big farmhouse in dire need of painting, and so engulfed in overgrown bush and gnarled apple trees it appeared to have sprouted straight out of the ground.

The kids always kept a wide berth around that farmhouse because of the old man who lived there. His name was Smith, they were told, and he owned all the property, including all of French Lake, and he had only half a tongue, chopped off in the war apparently, and couldn't speak properly. Smith, they said, had no objection to people picnicking on his property or swimming in his lake, as long as no one bothered him.

No one ever did. In fact, no one ever laid eyes on any person near or around that house, except Bob, who assured his sisters that the old guy most certainly was in there. Bob saw Smith once, peering evilly at him through the front window one day while Bob was picking berries by himself. It never occurred to the girls that the entire story might be a fabricated means of confining them to an allotted area, nor did they question Bob's account, despite his usual aversion to berry picking, alone or otherwise.

On that morning, Mary had the day's supplies packed and assembled on the front step: the propane cooking stove, the food, drinks, blankets, towels, hats, flip-flops, and the kids, all ready to be jammed into the car upon Fred's return from a "quick dash" to the Base.

And there they waited. Eventually, the sun's rays shortened and a shadow crept over the steps. Gradually, the kids wandered off to play in the neigbourhood, their bathing suits still under their clothes and, after a time, Mary put the food back in the fridge, still packed. Later, she put everything away, their days at the beach less and less predictable.

Since the family's return to Canada, all the outside pressures and strains of the past had been overcome, the sickness, the stressed in-law relations, as well as being so far from home for so long. Even money issues had eased. But in the wake of it all, Mary felt as if her and Fred's relationship had been left changed.

Mary viewed their posting to Germany as a kind of bridge, a means for her and Fred to find their way back to the companionship of their first few years as a couple. But now, although they were physically back, their relationship was not. Mary couldn't get her head around it; she pressed, and pushed, and fought hard, as was her way and still the intervals of peaceful harmony between the two of them shortened, while long, hurt silences or full out yelling matches lengthened.

Before their time on Nootka Street was over, though, the natural circle of life would intervene on Fred and Mary's behalf and set the two of them back on the road together.

Mary could not say she was surprised at the death of her father in 1966, and not simply because he was eighty-eight. Frankly, Dolph had always been an old man to her from their first days

83

together. But that had never mattered; he'd always had such a resolute strength about him, always defying in life the number of years on a calendar.

After returning from Germany, Mary travelled to Liverpool as soon as she was able to get there and was shocked at the change in Dolph. The gritty drive, so much a part of his character, had seeped away, and, according to her mum, it had been doing so since the day Joe died. Mary was grateful for her visits to Liverpool and Dolph's visits with Jeannette to her house in Oromocto. She would so miss that special bond she and her father shared. But she knew in her heart he was ready to go, and that in so many ways he had already gone.

Freddie was away, on course in Borden, Ontario, when Dolph died, but he, too, genuinely and deeply mourned his feisty old father-in-law. Dolph had always taken Fred's side, right from the start, imploring even Mary on occasion to "give the creature a break, Elizabeth." Mary longed for Fred's nearness in her sorrow, and when he finally made it home, she felt calmed and supported.

Two years later, in 1968, Mary returned the same kind of emotional comfort to Fred upon the death of his father. John-Tom died of a heart attack in his sleep at age seventy-four. The family's last photo of Grampy LeBlanc was of him sitting on the front step of their Nootka St. PMQ, squinting into the sunshine. He had been holding his newest grandchild. Frederick Louis LeBlanc (Louie) was born July 25, 1967, the last of Mary and Fred's five children.

21

ST. JOHN AVE. 1968 TO 1972

Louie was born into roaring times. By 1967, drugs, sex, and rock 'n' roll, or at least a version of that raving counter culture, had found an enthused concentration of followers in Oromocto, NB. The town was now filled to the brim with hormone-saturated baby boomer teenagers. By the time Louie was two years old, and the family had moved to a bigger house on St. John Avenue, all four of his siblings were officially among those ranks.

At that same time, another social phenomenon appeared to be adding to the dynamics within the Town of Oromocto, and for Mary and Fred in particular. For most children of military families, being called an "army brat" is a source of pride, one that evokes a feeling of a larger family, a shared communal experience, a way of life that draws strength in being independent, adaptable, and part of a supportive network.

In many quarters, however, that term was used in a much more literal sense, and, some thought, with good reason. In years past, outside a military community, the stereotypical "army brats" were often viewed as young people, teenagers mostly, who were out of control because of their chronically absentee fathers and the perceived weaker discipline tendencies of a female at the helm of the family.

Less recognized was the parenting style of military wives, who, in their effort to cope as the mostly lone parent of big families, tended to overcompensate with unrelenting control and discipline. Ironically, both types of extreme parenting produced the same kind of rebellious teen, and while both certainly did exist in Oromocto, in reality, it was nowhere near restricted to military kids, nor even to the 1960s.

In any case, in the LeBlanc household, it would be fair to say that Mary was a staunch member of that second camp, and, in keeping with an era that especially liked its labels, she and her two oldest teenagers were grappling with an intense "generation gap."

Mary could not, for the God-given life of her, understand what the problem was. She took her job as the mother seriously, deadly seriously. Since her illness, she had done everything she was supposed to for them, starting with always, always being there. They were involved in activities; Bobby especially liked hunting and fishing. There were school sports, swimming lessons, dance classes. They took annual summer vacations in Pictou, where, in the company of an entire town of Hawse, Currie, and LeBlanc cousins, the kids enjoyed relatively free reign.

And yet, here she was, locked in a growing power battle with both Bobby and Lee, heading to the boiling. Bobby was then, and had always been, the reigning monarch among his siblings, who, for the most part, were eager to please him as well as his wild friends whenever they were around. Bob's father's nickname for him would vacillate between "The Prodigal Son" or "Sir Robert," depending on the incident.

As a child, and even growing into adulthood, Bob was a complicated study in contradictions. He was hilarious, the most sharply witted of them all, but shy and self-conscious at the same time; he was intelligent and curious, but despised school with every fibre of his being; he cared deeply and gently, but angered with the speed

86

of light and was quick with his fists. His mother loved him with all that she had, but they fought constantly.

Outwardly, Mary blamed the bad influence of his friends for all the trouble he got into as a teen: frequent drinking, wild partying, refusing to go to school, smashing up or burning the motors out of various vehicles while his father was away. But inwardly, she agonized over how she might have done better, although she never did quite know what.

So, it was with relief for both Fred and Mary when, at age seventeen, the very day he was old enough, Bobby quit school and joined the army. The military would be the best thing for him, Mary and Fred hoped, give him some structure and discipline, while he earned a living at the same time. And Mary prayed that it would.

22

THE CULMINATION

Jackie and Annie hustled down the hill along the darkened walkway that led from the school to the parking lot area behind their St. John Avenue two-story PMQ. They were hurrying, hoping Mum wouldn't flip out altogether at the fact that they were late. She had been especially vigilant lately.

Gradually, the girls noticed an unusual amount of light coming from the parking lot, and as they got closer, they could see most of it whirling from the tops of a couple of Military Police cars. Also illuminated was Bobby, pie-eyed drunk, still in his army fatigues, swearing and swinging at two MPs, the "fuckin' meatheads," who were stuffing him in the back of one of the vehicles. Even more startling was the vision of their father, also in the parking lot, also being manhandled by a different pair of MPs, and also pie-eyed drunk, although Dad was wearing only underwear.

By this particular night, and this point in the LeBlanc family saga, the spring of 1971, Bob had been a couple of years in the army, posted to CFB Gagetown after his basic training. Now, he and his father were traveling loosely in the same work circles. As a result, the two occasionally found themselves together at alcohol imbibing functions, some compulsory, most voluntary. Sometimes Bob would arrive already buzzed, having spent his work day afternoon buying cans of beer that stocked the pop machines throughout base buildings. But both drank too much and, like a couple of adolescent pissing contestants, often ended their soirees engaged in full-on fights.

This one followed Freddie home. Luckily, the MPs were accustomed to drunken brawls and verbal abuse, especially involving young soldiers. A toss in the guardhouse for one or both combatants was about as far as they went, which is where Bobby landed that night. Mary, however, had become far less tolerant. She, in fact, had called the MPs herself after being unable to break up the melee that erupted in her kitchen.

The interlude of tranquility between Mary and Fred after the death of their fathers and the birth of their youngest child had gradually but significantly dissipated. Mary blamed the stress of dealing with headstrong teenagers for the increased turmoil. The relationship with her two oldest children was particularly fractious, marked by an accelerated fight for control. She had hoped, now that Bob was an adult in the military, episodes such as this one would have long ceased. That night, she let the MPs deal with those two "armpits." Frankly, Mary had far more important things to deal with at this juncture in their lives.

The previous year, 1970, had been the absolute height of it all for Mary, a culmination of sorts, and a trial for the entire family, rivalled only by the time of her illness. At seventeen, Lee had grown into a beautiful young woman. Physically, she was a mixture of both her parents: dark-haired, with her mother's fair complexion and high cheek bones, and her father's soft hazel eyes, a straight-lined nose and wide-winning smile. There was no shortage of young male teens who were attracted to Lee, but there was only one about whom she felt the same.

Dave Foster had originally been a friend of Bob. He lived in the same neighbourhood, one street over. Dave was a bit older than

Lee, though they were in the same grade. He was blond with deep-set amber eyes. For Lee, it was love at first sight. She fell hard and fast for his shy, self-conscious advances. In him, and in her innocence, she knew, as surely as she knew her own name, they had found each other's kindred spirit, forever.

Lee and Dave were heading into their high school graduation year and, like the times they were living in, the young couple were swept up into the wild, exciting, and carefree summer and fall of 1970. Dave had a car and they would often join the huge crowd of partiers at the local dump along the narrow River Road, where bonfires, drinking, smoking weed, dropping acid, and parking were the regular weekend pastimes. It was shortly before Christmas when Lee realized she was pregnant.

"I don't even remember telling Mum," Lee said decades later, recalling that traumatic time. "She just seemed to already know, somehow, and accepted that it happened. There wasn't any big blowout scene in the beginning."

Mary and Fred had indeed accepted the news with surprising calmness. It was far from the best time, for sure, but it was a story as old as time, and, of course, in Mary's and Fred's world, Lee and the baby's father would do what had always been done: they would get married.

Except, Lee was not living in Mary's and Fred's world. An automatic marriage, based simply on an unplanned pregnancy, was no longer the way things operated. It was 1971, after all, although society's new freedoms had yet to catch up with the simple facts of life, and the resulting explosion of teen pregnancies.

Mary was doing her best to deal with circumstances such as they were for their family. After coming to terms with the fact that Lee and Dave would not be getting married, Mary came up with

90

plan B. Lee would finish school, have the baby, and get a job. She and the baby could live at home until such time as Lee could afford for the two of them to live on their own. Mary would help her as much as she could with babysitting and other chores, even though she still had her own toddler at home.

There would be one condition, however, and it was solidly unmovable. If Dave Foster was not willing to step up in his responsibilities, Lee would not be permitted to have anything at all to do with him, so long as she lived under their roof. She would have to choose, him or them. Lee was her mother's child, and dug in for the fight, equally unmovable. She chose him.

Shortly into the new year, Lee packed her bags and moved in with the Fosters, one street over. It was a decision she would soon regret, much sooner than any of her own family ever realized. Dave's mother was not happy with the arrangement and only begrudgingly allowed Lee to live there, making no bones about her feelings.

Lee's situation with the Fosters was by no means improved when Fred arrived at their door in a last-ditch attempt to persuade Lee to come home. There were two things wrong with Fred's negotiation style, however. The first was that he had had a few swigs beforehand, which was likely the cause of the fisticuffs that broke out between him and Dave's father. Secondly, and no doubt the real reason for the failure of the effort, there appeared to be no change in Fred's and Mary's fundamental terms. In the absence of Dave Foster "doing the right thing," there would be no Dave Foster in their lives.

The hot summer rolled on, and in the early hours of August 18, 1971, exactly one week before her eighteenth birthday, Lee gave birth to a baby boy. By that time, she and Dave had broken up, and

91

Lee was working as a live-in nanny in the Fredericton area while Dave was preparing to move west.

Neither Mary nor Fred were aware that Lee and Dave were no longer a couple, only that she was not living with the Fosters, and Lee had no intention of giving her parents any more ammunition against Dave than they already had, together or not. At the hospital, Fred and Mary's seething anger at Dave Foster and his family only deepened when they learned that Lee had signed the child's adoption papers. They assumed her feelings for Dave were unchanged and that she did it because of him. They were partly right.

Despite everything, Lee was not ready to let go of Dave Foster. Nearly a year later, she followed him to Calgary, where, eventually, she realized and finally accepted the fact that their whirlwind relationship was over. She and her parents ultimately made amends, but all three laboured long after with guilt and regret over what they should or should not have done. It was only through the passage of years that it would become clear to Mary and Fred, and to Lee herself, that on that hot summer day in August 1971, she really had done the right thing for her child.

Twenty years later, after agonized searching to no avail, right around Mother's Day, as implausibly corny as it may sound, Lee answered the phone to hear the voice of that baby boy, grown into a young man. He introduced himself as Jason Harding. Eventually, the whole family would meet him. He was the spitting image of Dave Foster.

23

GRANDKIDS

On January 1, 1972, the city of Fredericton, NB, celebrated its first baby of the new year. Penny Nadine LeBlanc was also the first baby for her parents, Mr. and Mrs. Bob and Cathy LeBlanc.

The year before, Bobby, at twenty, had married a young woman from Pictou. Cathy Murdock was funny and personable, a typical "down home" girl. Her hair was long and dark and Jackie and Annie were fascinated when she straightened it with the clothes iron, stretched out along the ironing board like a shining black wrap. They liked her, partly because she occupied that mysterious grey area between themselves and full adulthood. Most important for Mary, though, was the fact that this young woman had been the one and only force on earth who had the ability to slow Bobby down, to subdue the devils that chased him, at least for a time.

The new baby went by her middle name, Nadine, a beautiful child with bouncing rolls of blond hair. She was smart and chatty early on and photographed those first few years to within an inch of her life, Mary and Fred like a couple of possessed paparazzi. For them, the little girl embodied the gift of grandparenthood: so much joy and love, so little work and worry.

Mary was still very much a parent herself. She had two teenage girls, Jackie and Annie, and a six-year-old, Louie, to work for and worry over. Lee was living in Alberta, where she had a good job and ended up staying to raise her own family.

In Oromocto, Mary was determined there would be no repeat of the earlier, harrowing teen saga. Between peacekeeping tours or field exercises, Mary enlisted Fred's help to tighten an already significantly battened down household, especially regarding the two teenage girls still at home. Fred would play the bad cop, which he appeared to think he was. Any sign of a skinny, pimpled, long-haired male circling anywhere near the LeBlancs' was met by Fred with open hostility, much to the mortification of Annie and Jackie.

"I don't know about you birds," he was known to spout in baritone on the step of their Laurier Drive PMQ, "but we eat around here at 5:00 o'clock. Fly the hell home."

A simple "time for supper" might have sufficed, and initially the boys did fly, but if they were brave, or perhaps stunned enough to continue the stalk, they soon figured out what those close to Fred already knew.

On the surface, Mary and Fred invariably presented an Archie and Edith Bunker façade, Fred spewing a litany of gruff orders and/or politically incorrect commentary and running jokes, with Mary the subservient little woman. The couple played their traditional roles convincingly for anyone on the outside looking in. But it was largely a farce, even if they didn't recognize it themselves. Ultimately, the boys would come to know, the one person in that duo to be truly leery of was never Fred.

"Holy shit," Annie said to Jackie one Saturday night on Laurier Drive, keeping her voice low in their dimly lit living room. "She must be dead to the world. We've been sitting here, what, fifteen minutes?"

The girls had just arrived home from a teen dance. They were late. Explicit instructions had been to be in the house by the stroke of midnight like two teeny-bopper Cinderellas. That meant they

94

had to leave the dance early to make it from the community centre to Laurier Drive on time, a fifteen-minute brisk walk, or a seven-minute dash.

Had it not been for the two young gentlemen who graciously offered to escort them home, the girls might have made curfew that night. One was tall and fair, the other shorter and dark, both gangly in their high riding bell bottoms, platform shoes, and flowing shoulder length hair. The boys had purposely dilly-dallied, the two of them under no constraints to be anywhere specific, anytime soon. They even convinced the sisters, now that they had arrived at the darkened house, that it might be a good idea to let them come in and sit awhile. Likely their mother wouldn't mind, especially since they were now home safe and sound, eh?

There the four of them sat that night, the girls nervous, surprised Mum hadn't met them at the door steaming mad, the boys unaware of exactly how wrong their assessment of Mrs. LeBlanc was. Within minutes, a clearer picture hit home when the small woman flew in the front door, her hair wind-blown and askew, wearing a three-quarter length jacket over a full-length plaid housecoat and a pair of all-weather ankle boots. She had not been sleeping, as the boys had hoped: she had been out, gone to retrieve her girls at 12:05, on foot since she didn't drive. Somehow, by the mercy of God, the girls had not crossed paths with their mother in public, neither at the dance nor on their way home.

Jackie's and Annie's guests realized quickly this was no regular-level pissed-off mum and took off in a blur after Mrs. LeBlanc's menacingly quiet instruction to "Go, now."

To their under-recognized credit, those boys never did go far. They stayed clear of Mary initially, circumventing and wangling around all her rules and regulations, but within a few years, they both would be husbands to the LeBlanc sisters, and there would be three more grandchildren for Mary and Fred, including Bobby and Cathy's second child.

Despite Mary's herculean efforts, or maybe because of them, her two youngest daughters had become teenage brides and mothers, both too young to be either. Yet both managed, with those same lads, to hang in for the long haul.

24

CFB CHATHAM

It was getting on to 2:00 A.M. one early Sunday morning, when Jackie's wall phone rang in the kitchen of her Tweedsmuir Court row house. Jackie had been sitting at the table, reading and sipping juice after finally getting her three-month-old girl resettled. This second infant's sleep cycle was proving far more difficult than her first baby boy, and, even though Jackie was exhausted, on that night she could not get back to sleep.

The phone startled her. "Jack?" said her father's deep pitch.

"Dad?" she answered surprised. "What's the matter, what's happened?"

"Listen, Jack," Fred carried on hurriedly, "don't worry, everything is all right," which confirmed, if the middle of the night phone call hadn't, there was something to worry about.

"We're here at the Oromocto Hospital. We had a small car accident coming through Sheffield. Mum is going to be admitted here."

"Jesus. Is she all right? Is Louie all right?"

"Louie is fine, a little shaken up, but they think Mum has a cracked pelvis."

Questions burst in Jackie's mind right then, starting with what in hell they were doing across the river in Sheffield that late at night. Especially given the fact that her parents and

97

younger brother no longer lived in Oromocto. They now lived in northeastern New Brunswick, two hundred kilometres away.

About a year earlier, 1976, after fourteen years in Oromocto, Fred requested and was granted a posting to Chatham. CFB Chatham had originally functioned as a Canadian Air Force base. Although it continued to operate largely in that realm, in the late 1960s that base, along with all the others across the country, had integrated all three branches of the Canadian Forces, which was why an infantry soldier such as Fred could be stationed there.

The posting had been a huge decision for Mary, one she did not take lightly. When Jackie and Annie had become young mothers, both girls leaned heavily on her. Mary knew the stresses and adjustments for them were enormous and she was happy to help them get started. But soon Mary felt as if she was not only raising her own child still at home, but also her grandchildren. Moving to Chatham meant that, while she would be close enough to see the kids often, she would no longer be on day to day call.

There was something else in play for Mary, something that was only just beginning to gel in her consciousness. Space away from her grown children, from the hustle and bustle of a constantly busy household in Oromocto, might create a place where she and Fred could lead a less frenetic life for once, one where the two of them could reconnect and move forward in a calmer, quieter environment. Fred needed less stress in his life. As far as Mary was concerned, his last tour was proof.

Towards the end of 1974, Canadian soldiers had been deployed to the Suez Canal's west bank near the city of Ismailia in Egypt. UN peacekeeping forces had been sent to man the buffer zone area established between Egypt and Israel at the end of the 1973 Arab-Israeli conflict. Fred, with his unit, was scheduled to be there for

98

six months, but within a week of their arrival, after finishing up an early shift and preparing for an off-duty sightseeing drive to Cairo, someone asked Fred if he was feeling okay. It was the last thing he remembered prior to waking up in the field unit's equivalent of intensive care. Fred was then medevacked to a facility in Germany, stabilized, and sent back to the Atlantic CF Health Services in Halifax for a month of intense medical investigations. Fortunately, no residual or ongoing issues could be found, other than a sky-rocketed blood pressure episode. Treated for that and declared fit for duty, Fred returned to Gagetown and shortly thereafter took the posting to Chatham.

Louie was nearly eight years old when they moved, and all the reasons Mary and Fred had for wanting to go were exactly why Lou would have preferred to stay. Chatham was a much smaller community, he didn't know anyone, and he missed his old school, his old friends, and the hustle and bustle of that constantly busy house in Oromocto.

Unfortunately, the less hectic, more peaceful existence Mary was convinced she and Fred needed appeared to be as elusive as ever in Chatham. Without their adult kids and grandkids around frequently, she and Fred simply had more time and opportunity to argue and bicker. Again, during those last few years in Oromocto, Fred had gradually returned to his old pattern of drinking and absence from her and Louie's lives, over and above his work or tours of duty.

In Chatham their relationship and family life did not improve. It actually grew worse, far worse than the most difficult point in their relationship years ago on Nootka Street. This time the loneliness Mary felt was deeper, and was now tinged by a feeling of dread and hopelessness.

99

By that late summer night, on the narrow road in Sheffield, Mary, Fred and Louie had been living in Chatham for a year and were returning home from a vacation in Pictou during Fred's annual leave. It was about a week and a half earlier than the two weeks they planned to stay. In Pictou, on the first day of their holiday, Fred immediately embarked on a three-day bender after he dropped Mary and Louie off at his mother's place like a couple of bags of luggage. By the third day, after Fred woke up but before he could get started again, Mary demanded he take them home right then and there. She packed up; she was not staying, not one more night.

Hence the reason for the three of them being on the old 105 Highway near Sheffield at that time of the night. They were four hours into a six-hour trip back to northeastern New Brunswick when the effects of Fred's last binge caught up with him. He fell asleep at the wheel of their '67 Volkswagen Bug. Two things likely saved one or all of their lives. The first was that there was no oncoming traffic on the two-lane road at the time that Fred unconsciously crossed to the other side. The second was the gigantic maple tree that halted the vehicle's trajectory straight into the Saint John River.

The car hit the tree mostly on Mary's passenger side, easily crumpling the front-end boot of the VW, and hurling Fred completely through the windshield. Fred remembered nothing about the accident, other than waking up outside the vehicle. Unbelievably, his only injuries consisted of bruising that showed up days later. Louie and their small dog, both of whom were sleeping under a blanket in the back seat, also sustained no injuries other than minor bruising. Only Mary was hurt, a cracked pelvis the doctors determined at the hospital.

People living in the area called the police and ambulance immediately. The next day the local paper featured a short article headlined, "Doze Causes Mishap," which was good for a small chuckle, especially after the family realized Mary would recoup fully, the crack in her hip actually a hairline fracture.

Mary, however, was not laughing. Neither was she yelling, arguing, or pleading. A measure of the quiet calm she sought had finally come. She was done.

25

DONE

Every one of the significant men in Mary's life, her father, all five brothers, her husband, and even her oldest son, had been cut from a similar swatch of cloth. They worked hard, her men, but they played hard too, and each one, to varying degrees, had a definite bend toward the wild side. Mary loved them all deeply and thoroughly, but ingrained in her upbringing was the underlying idea that males in general required an extra layer of help in a perpetual struggle against themselves, the kind that only a strong female could provide. It had been her life's calling from the time she was five.

That personal history may have been the reason it took twenty years, and a car accident, for Mary to realize that Fred's drinking was not about coping with their situational problems and circumstances, certainly not at this point. Drinking was Fred's go-to response for everything, Mary now realized in full clarity. Whether he was happy, sad, stressed, relaxed, bored, or busy, all required the frequent release of a tied-on drunk. The accident in Sheffield was the catalyst that ultimately crystalized for Mary what all the noise and racket, the trials and tribulations, had masked: Fred was a bona fide alcoholic, a serious binge drinker and there was nothing she could say or do that had not already been said and done to make him stop.

Back home in Chatham, Mary prepared to leave Fred. It was a decision that strained the very fabric of who she was as a person. She would be relinquishing, she knew, not only her place and purpose in the world as a wife, but the fundamental sense of security she felt at being specifically a military wife.

"I liked being an army wife," Mary mused years later. "I always thought, you know, deep down, that if the worst were ever to come, the military would take care of us."

Even so, Mary determined she would be moving forward on her own. Her decision had nothing to do with her feelings for Fred. Those would never change. He was then, and would always be, the love of her life. But there was another male in her life, too, one who trumped even Fred, and there was another role she had, one more important than being a wife. She was still the mother of her youngest son, Louie.

"By that time, Bobby was really having a hard go," Mary later remembered. "He and Cathy had split up because of his drinking and I just thought that if I didn't make that move, Lou was going to end up like the two of them. I didn't see it when Bob was young, but I saw it clear as a bell then."

For most of the years that Fred had been in the Armed Forces, support services for the families of military members were few and far between. In fact, early on, any conflicts that spilled beyond the family circle could negatively impact that member's career. Problems were expected to be dealt with at home, when home, by the soldier. Families in military communities were left to deal with the serious challenges of separation, isolation, the absence of extended family support, the inability to set down roots, and the lack of higher education and employment for spouses on their own. In the mid-1970s, however, official military culture slowly began

103

to evolve. Today, Military Family Resource Centres across the country attempt to address the unique challenges of military life, recognizing that supporting the soldier's family is one of the best ways to support the soldier.

During Mary's time in Chatham, Mary knew of only one general counselling office open to military family members, housed in a tiny grey room tucked in an out of the way corner on base. Most wives, if they were even aware it existed, avoided it like the plague, convinced that anything they might be grappling with would be translated directly from that office to their spouse's commanding officer. A person would have to be pretty much desperate to go anywhere near it.

Mary did, and, in the end, she was right. When that indefinable worst had come and she had accepted the fact that she had lost her husband "to the bottle altogether," it was the military who assured her that she and Louie would indeed be taken care of.

The counsellor she spoke to that day was a young man, the base's social work officer, who looked to Mary to be about twelve.

"I remember thinking, 'My cripes, how in hell is this kid gonna help me or anybody?' He looked like he needed his mother himself."

She was wrong. Ultimately, the baby-faced young man not only saved her marriage and her family unit, but he also may have saved Fred. He did not, however, advise Mary to stay. The exact opposite. He began by explaining the insidious nature of a gripping alcohol addiction, the many forms it can take, from the excessive binge drinker to the everyday boozer. There were functioning and non-functioning alcoholics, he explained, and everything in between. But the thing all addicts had in common was the devastating, long-term effects on themselves and those close to them.

104

Without some kind of serious intervention in Fred's addictive behaviour, she could count on the problems only getting worse.

Rather than seeing herself as a failure for her inability to get Fred to stop drinking or slow down, the social worker helped her see that, by staying, she may very well empower him to continue. He also told her that the law would require Fred to support her and their son financially, and that, as long as Fred was in the military, the Canadian Armed Forces would see to it that Fred did, even if they had to garnish his wages. At this point, the young man reassured Mary that she was right to pursue her own path, for her son's sake, for her sake, and even for Fred's.

Mary was frightened, but in 1977 in Chatham, she prepared for a seismic shift in her world.

Not long after that counseling session, the girls came up from Oromocto, along with their husbands and kids. They stayed the night, as they occasionally did, looking forward to a round of cribbage, a laugh, a gab. But by their return home on Sunday most of the normal routine they had come to expect hadn't happened. Mum seemed miles away, quiet, disengaged.

Their husbands, too, had gotten used to Fred's sarcastic, buzzed banter, always good for a chuckle. But on this weekend, although he was drinking, Fred seemed unusually sullen, dark. He and the boys went to the "mess" on base that Saturday night. The three of them were sitting around a table when Fred suddenly drained his double rye-whisky, took direct aim at the largest, most menacing person in the place, and deliberately whizzed the empty glass just past his head. Fred then casually stood, pointed to his two shocked sons-in-law, and took off, leaving them to deal with the aftermath. Somehow, they managed to talk themselves out of the place with their faces still intact. Back at the house, they discovered Fred had walked home and gone to bed.

Fred was seething angry, of that there was no doubt, but at what or whom exactly he had yet to figure out. He had found the papers, the forms, and the information pamphlets, the ones Mary had been given by the counsellor. It wasn't that Mary had tried to hide the documents, but neither had she openly discussed anything with Fred about a separation. The time for talking, at least on Mary's part, had long passed and Fred could clearly see her standing firm at a crossroad in his life, with her bags packed.

"It was true," Fred said, simply, years later, "they were alone, and as long as I was drinking, Lou was growing up without a father."

Fred insisted to Mary that he could stop drinking, and that he would stop, and asked for one chance to prove it. She gave him that chance, and thus, nearly forty years after he, Peter Gallant, and the Elliot brothers had tasted their first bitter swig of "74 Dark" at age thirteen, Fred LeBlanc quit drinking. He did it cold turkey, relying solely on his strength of will, and Mary.

"Alcoholics Anonymous, and all that kind of thing," said Fred, "that wasn't something I was ever gonna do. I figured when a person decides they need to do something, they just have to do it."

A simple strategy, and it did work for Fred, although it was far from a simple process. The effects of withdrawal were visible to anyone who knew Fred, as well as a few who didn't. He was edgy, anxious, often outright cantankerous, and, most revealing at the time, Fred turned down a posting to Kingston, Ontario, one that would have come with a promotion.

"I only had a few years left before my twenty-five-year pension," Fred said about his decision. "Going to Ontario just wasn't worth it

106

for me then, taking on something that new, and trying to stay on the wagon. It wouldn't have made much difference in money anyway."

Fred chose to forego full-sergeant stripes in exchange for his last two years at the small military station CFS Debert, Nova Scotia, once known as "the Diefenbunker." Most importantly for Fred, Debert was only forty-five minutes from his home and anchor, Pictou. Mary and Fred bought a Heights house on Poplar Street. in Pictou, fixed it up, and rented it out until their final permanent return.

By which time, slowly, gradually, the more deeply authentic, admirable, and lovable Freddie re-emerged for Mary; the impatient, sarcastic, funny, relentlessly rude Freddie, in all his one-liner glory, even sharper sober.

26

THE PIANO

The ultimate test of Fred's new-found sobriety came with the death of his mother, Johanna, in 1978. It was a blow, but he struggled through it, managed to maintain his abstinence, and felt good about the fact that, before she died, Johanna did see the start of her son's lasting new lease on life.

At eighty-two, Johanna had declined significantly and had been admitted to a nursing home. Even there, the outspoken little woman managed to make her sharpened opinions known, requesting to be promptly shot if she ever appeared wearing more than one dress at a time and somebody else's dentures.

Fred remembered Johanna's trips to Oromocto all those years, travelling in his fixer-up vehicles, the blur of the road she swore she could see through the holes in the floor, the back seat so cold her blanket had stiffened into the shape of her knees, the rattling racket from the car's loose and "laughing fenders": Johanna's specialty, complaints in the form of hilarious commentary, the thing they would all miss most.

None of that was what Mary remembered the most. Over the years, Johanna and Mary had forged a relationship, despite the power struggle that had erupted between them early on. They had come to respect one another through their common emotional ground—their love for Fred and the kids—and, in the end, Mary was left wondering whether or not Johanna knew how grateful she was for all her mother-in-law had done for them so long ago.

Johanna's death made Mary realize, too, a deeper appreciation for her own mum, one that strengthened as Jeannette slipped. Now into her seventies, Jeannette was suffering from serious memory loss. Soon she would be diagnosed with arteriosclerosis, a "hardening of the arteries" type dementia, progressing to the point where she was placed in a home in Liverpool close to most of her boys and their families.

Mary and Fred often made the day trip to see her from Pictou, and Mary worried that one day she would arrive to Jeannette not knowing who she was. It never happened. Invariably, Jeannette would call her name, excited to see her, even though she would forget within minutes the gift Mary had brought or the fact that they were not visiting in Mary's house. Her memory was usually either in the here and now or in the long ago, and sometimes a garbled mixture of both, but as she had her entire life, Jeannette truly enjoyed all visitors all the time.

Jeannette also continued to love her music, the soundtrack of Prince Edward Island, fiddles and spoons, keyboards and guitar, the kind that moved her to sing and step whenever she heard it. Mary watched her mum, tapping and singing along with the group who had come to the nursing home to entertain, and marveled that Jeannette had zero recollection of the last ten minutes, but hardly missed a word of the familiar old tunes.

Of all the gifts in life Jeannette had so freely given, Mary realized during those visits, that would be the most enduring: the gift of music. Not the ability to play or sing, Jeannette was never known for her actual talent, but the sheer joy and colour of music, symbolized by an old stand-up piano, huge and heavy, an heirloom from Mary's adolescence.

It is puzzling why the Gallants bought such a thing at the time in their lives that they did, living in their small Heights house in Pictou. No one could play the piano, then, and certainly the Gallants were never known to spend Dolph's hard-earned money on anything remotely frivolous or impractical. They didn't even have a car. But they did buy that huge piano, and Mary did have a knack for it, as it turned out, doggedly teaching herself to pick out basic chords, eventually moving to full tunes, all purely by ear, and all to Jeannette's complete delight.

Around the same time that the Gallants acquired the piano, not long after moving to Pictou, Jeannette finally yielded to Mary's probing questions about her biological mother. Whether that piano was meant as a deliberate distraction for Mary is hard to guess, but, forever after those two disparate things, the piano and the questions, always seemed to emerge concurrently in Mary's memory.

Mary was twelve at the time and she was grappling with having left their Island home. New had never been much of a difficulty for Mary. Eventually, she adjusted to almost anywhere and anything that came her way. However, the act of leaving invariably stirred and churned Mary's deeply ingrained anxieties. This major relocation expressed itself in the form of an interrogation of Jeannette, a re-dredged refrain about what was left behind in PEI. Was Mary's real mother still back there? Would she be there when they returned to the Island? Did she have more kids after she got married? And, as always, why did her real mother give her away?

At this point, Jeannette knew there could be no fudging the narrative. Mary was too smart for that, and although she couldn't give her the answers to everything, Jeannette resolved it was time to tell Mary all that she did know.

110

Mary's biological mother's name was Adeline Whitty. That much Mary already knew. Jeannette wasn't sure if Adeline was still living near Souris with the man she had married or not. Neither did she know the name of Adeline's husband, but she did tell Mary about the rumour, according to old Aunt Genevieve, that Adeline may have had another child, a boy. Aunt Gen was gone now, but had lived most of her married life in Souris. The whisper she heard was that Adeline had a son, younger than Mary, although he had never lived at any time with his biological mother or any of the McIntoshes. Who or where he was, or if he really existed, Jeannette did not know.

Jeannette realized there was no way to soften the fundamental fact that Mary's biological mother was an unmarried woman, which meant that Mary, and possibly another child, had been born "illegitimate" children. Their mother had no means of looking after either one of them, Jeannette explained gently, and Mary must remember that those were very hard times for a lot of people who lived in the townships on PEI. As for who her biological father was or why he couldn't have provided for them, Jeannette honestly could not tell her.

Mary remembered being totally dumbfounded. Try as she might, she had never been able to conjure up anything more than a few snippets of memory, a grainy old movie reel flickering in her head, one that never quite captured her biological mother's face. Now she had two more faces to concoct in her mind, a brother and a father.

The old piano was in rough shape by the time Jeannette had given up her house for the nursing home. Mary claimed it, and had it moved to her place. It had been functioning mostly as a gigantic picture and plant stand those last years. The inside

111

strings hung loose or were snapped entirely, the keys chipped, browned, and cracked like aged fingernails. Mary refurbished it, paying for a complete replacement of the inside along with a new set of keys and foot-peddles. Then, by hand, she scraped and sanded for months, layers and years of paint and yellowed varnish, totally refinishing the outside woodwork, only to have the job entirely redone professionally.

For Mary, that old piano held her past, before the kids, before the sickness, before Fred and, on some level, even before Dolph and Jeannette. Through those keys, Prince Edward Island itself beckoned.

27

THE SEARCH BEGINS

In 1979, Mary and Fred moved back to Pictou after nearly thirty years. Although the same two people officially returned, a very different couple had come home, worn around the edges and wiser. Mary and Fred's relationship had been mending, and their return to Pictou reflected it.

Fred became a civilian, working a Monday to Friday job as facility manager of the Highlander Reserve Armoury, the long tours and endless absences behind them. Louie settled well into junior high school in Pictou, his "new kid" status eased by the fact that he was related, by blood or marriage, to a sizeable number of the town's population. And, of course, all four of Mary's and Fred's older kids had long been on their own, busily producing and raising grandchildren. It was within this space and time of relative calm that Mary, as her own person, emerged; old interests became new, and old yearnings were fully freed.

The piano was tuned and singing. Even Fred tried to learn to play and keep time on the mandolin, most often, mercifully, drowned out by the better talent assembled on a Saturday night. In later years, Mary joined an all-female band made up of singers, a fiddler, guitar players, and herself on keyboard. They practiced weekly, and volunteered as often as possible for nursing homes and other small venues, calling themselves The Forget Me Nots.

Playing in the band was the most rewarding activity Mary

113

enjoyed just for herself, independent of Fred and the family, except for a niece, a member of the band who, along with a talented old friend, Helen Marks, had coaxed her into joining.

Mary stayed with the group well into her eighties, snickering along with everyone else every time Fred referred to them as The Will Nots.

Back in Pictou, Fred and Mary's bond had tightened. They were moving forward again, secured to what had originally cemented them as kids: their friendship. They renewed their wedding vows, again at the Stella Maris, this time surrounded by their children and grandchildren. Bob did point out, though, that technically he was also at the first wedding. And, Mary told Fred, she'd let him know at the altar whether or not she was going to say "I do" a second time.

Except for her two boys and their children, Mary was again immersed in a town full of Fred's gigantic extended family. After the death of her mum in 1992, Mary only occasionally saw her own siblings. Her one sister, Laura, lived in BC, and three of her four brothers were still in Liverpool. Her youngest brother, Winston, the baby of the Gallant family, however, decided to retire in Pictou.

Mary was ecstatic. He fit in with the LeBlancs as if the forty years since he had lived in Pictou had never happened. Easily, Winston slipped into Peter Gallant's old spot as Fred's best chum—minus the drinking, smoking, and chasing girls. Years before, Winston had also beaten a serious alcohol addiction. He was single again by this time in his life, and Mary showered him with the attention she always did when he was a boy and she was charged with keeping him out of trouble. In the end, Mary and Winston were the only two Gallant siblings left, and their appreciation of each other strengthened.

114

It was also at this point in Mary's life, not long after moving back to Pictou, that she and Fred embarked on a quest to find Mary's long-lost Island people. It was exciting, hopeful, and scary all at once for Mary, but it was time, she knew, and she loved Fred even more for being as invested as she was in the search. On a breezy summer day in 1983, they boarded an early morning ferry to Prince Edward Island. Mary's stomach rolled in sync with the boat. She was feeling lightheaded, the gas fumes from the car deck thinning as they made their way to the open air above.

Unlike her husband, Mary never did like boats. Strange, she thought, for a life that had been so shaped by proximity to the sea. They were heading to Souris.

The search had begun months before in their Heights house kitchen with a review of what Mary already knew for certain. At the time of Mary's birth, Adeline Whitty lived in the Souris East Lighthouse with her paternal aunt, Christina McIntosh, along with Christina's husband, Frank, the lighthouse keeper, and their eleven children. Adeline possibly had another child, a son. At some point, Adeline had died.

The plan for the trip was two-fold. Fred had made arrangements to meet with Father Edwin Steele, the presiding priest at St. Mary's Catholic Church in Souris. He agreed to help the couple with a search of parish records. The Whittys and McIntoshes were devout Catholics, and like Catholic rectories the world over, St. Mary's kept detailed lists of all parishioners' births, deaths, baptisms, and marriages.

They also planned to call on Christina McIntosh. Of all the characters in the story of Mary's mysterious first five years, Christina had always loomed the largest in Mary's mind. Mary

115

remembered her, and not just an imagined version. She saw Christina twice after she left the lighthouse. Both times, Christina had initiated the contact, first at the Gallant farm when Mary was seven, and many years later on Nootka St. in Oromocto. Christina had been in Oromocto once, visiting her son who was briefly stationed there.

Neither of those interactions had done much more than evoke further questions and both, in different ways, had left Mary with a generalized anxiousness, a disturbance that bubbled from her deepest core, one she still struggled to make sense of as a grown woman with children of her own.

Maybe if the circumstances at the time had been better, Mary thought, Christina's visit at her house in Oromocto had lasted hardly long enough for tea and a snack. The kids were young and had been running in and out, and Christina seemed intent on keeping the occasion light, a casual social call. Mary firmly believed that Christina had been a significant figure in the saga of Mary's early life, and that she knew more than she was willing to say. In Oromocto, there wasn't time or opportunity to push and dig, to ask or begin to understand the most pressing, burning question of all. Why? Why did her mother give her up at five years old?

And maybe, Mary admitted to herself, she hadn't been ready to know.

28

ANSWERS

St. Mary's Catholic Church in Souris is located on an expanse of green acreage overlooking the Souris River on the north end of town. The church is well over a century old, recorded as "Gothic" in design and laid out in the shape of a crucifix. Its pew capacity is twelve hundred, big enough to hold every man, woman, and child in Souris. The building is constructed almost entirely of PEI sandstone, with three huge front entrances of thick maple between two imposing towers.

It was noon when Fred and Mary arrived. They pulled the car around and entered through the less daunting side door of the church leading into the rectory. Father Steele was expecting them. He had done some preliminary work for the couple after Fred's phone call and was excited to show them the record of birth and baptism he found for a Richard Whitty, born August 2, 1933; mother, Adeline Whitty; and godmother, Mrs. M. F. McIntosh, Christina. The child's father's name had been listed "unknown." Father Steele was also surprised to find a copy of Richard Whitty's marriage certificate filed at St. Mary's.

Unfortunately, they realized, none of the records revealed Richard's adopted name, nor where Richard and his wife lived, and St. Mary's had no other information under Richard's birth name or the maiden name of Richard's wife. However, it did tell them at what church the couple had been married in 1960, the Immaculate

Conception Catholic Church in St. Louis, PEI. That was near Tignish, at the opposite end of the Island.

Fred thought it might be worthwhile to look into Catholic orphanages or adoption agencies operating on the Island at that time too. Richard might have gone through one of them. Father Steele agreed, although he did caution that there might be "issues" with that, especially given "the sensitive nature of their inquiries," code for the offensiveness of being born outside established sanctity. Many adoption agencies didn't even keep the old records of illegitimate children, he said, though they did for orphans of married parents.

"Cripes," Mary thought, "sensitive nature? Way past that now, bud." But, aloud, Mary thanked the priest politely and sincerely. They were certainly going to look into the church up Tignish way.

While they were in Souris, Mary and Fred were determined to talk to Christina. Fred had tracked down Rudy McIntosh, one of Christina's sons, and spoken to him in person. He was friendly and eager to help Mary's cause. He had always known about Adeline and little "Lizzie," everyone did, but the existence of Richard was a total shock to him. Christina had kept her secrets well.

Rudy directed the couple to the house the McIntoshes had moved to after the lighthouse, nearly fifty years prior. Christina was still there, by then well into her nineties, although she was still mentally sharp, Rudy said. He called ahead to the caregiver. Christina would be glad to see them.

Again, Mary was gripped by a vague and unbidden apprehension, as she and Fred were ushered into her biological great-aunt's living room. Christina was arranged neatly in a semi-recliner. She looked so much smaller than Mary recalled, thin, her hair totally white, her

118

face gaunt and patchy with age. But the eyes, they were the same.

"Lizzie." Christina extended a small, curled hand, and Mary took it. "You look like me."

Mary relaxed some. She would ask her questions, dig for the answers, knowing this would likely be Christina's final account of the story of Adeline Whitty's short life.

Adeline was born in Souris in 1912. Her parents, John and Julia Whitty, had eight children, seven girls and one boy. Adeline's father scraped along, as most Islanders did, farming, lumbering in the winter and a bit of fishing. Occasionally, in townships such as Souris, labour jobs here and there helped to fill the gaps.

When Adeline was fourteen, her mother died of tuberculosis, "consumption," Christina called it. At that point, as was very often the case when the mother of a household died, Adeline and her sisters were placed in homes, some of them with relatives, earning their keep as live-in help. Adeline went to the already crowded household of her paternal aunt, Christina McIntosh.

During the Depression years, Christina McIntosh's husband was among the few in Souris who had a decent steady income. Frank's job as the lighthouse keeper included free housing, and he also received a First World War veteran's pension. Christina, who had been a widow with three older children when she married Frank, was a fervently religious woman, staunchly Catholic. Often, she offered their home to relatives who found themselves in need of temporary sanctuary during those desperate Depression years.

Adeline, however, was permanent. She helped out around the McIntoshes, primarily responsible for the household's huge laundry duties. As she got older, Adeline took outside day jobs whenever the opportunity arose, sometimes including short periods away, but her home base was always with the McIntoshes.

119

At age seventeen, Adeline became pregnant out of wedlock. It was a shock to Christina, horrifically scandalous, and she struggled with what to do about the situation. Adeline was a jovial, fun-loving girl with a great sense of humour. But she was also extremely gullible, easily manipulated, and Christina felt Adeline had been taken advantage of, especially in light of the fact that she had lost her own mother's influence at such a young age.

Adeline's baby girl, christened Mary Elizabeth Whitty, was incorporated into the McIntosh household. Adeline and her daughter shared the same bed and "Lizzie" grew to play with the younger McIntosh kids in the house, or followed her mother around as Adeline carried out her duties.

Three years later, Adeline became pregnant again. She was now a twenty-one-year-old unwed woman, functionally illiterate, with very little opportunity to provide for herself, never mind two children. This second pregnancy was unknown to many of the McIntoshes, although Christina knew. As Father Steele had revealed, Christina was present at the birth of the baby boy and the infant's immediate Catholic baptism. The child was then sent to an orphanage in Charlottetown for adoption.

Nearly two years later, Lizzie was also given up, to the Gallants. Adeline's prospects had not improved any, although she continued to live with the McIntoshes after Lizzie left, even after Frank's tenure as the lighthouse keeper ended and the McIntosh family's eventual move to another home in Souris. Adeline lived with them until her marriage at age twenty-five to an older man, Edward Holland. He lived just outside Souris with his teenaged son, who was described simply as an "eccentric" boy.

That was when, shortly before Adeline was married, Christina made that trip to the Gallants' home in St. Georges with the intention of bringing Lizzie back to Souris to live with her mother and new husband, and was met with Dolph's categorical no. Three years later, at age twenty-eight, Adeline (Whitty) Holland died at home of pulmonary tuberculosis. She had suffered immensely at the end, in pain and full of bedsores.

Christina told the story matter-of-factly, laying out in cold chronology the tragic events that carried away the young woman's life like a tide. It seemed surreal to Mary, with gaps and pieces missing, things Mary asked about then and pondered long after. Christina cared for Adeline, that much was obvious in all that she had done for her niece, and in how much Adeline had confided in and depended on her aunt. So, Mary thought, it was unlikely that Christina would have no idea as to who the father of Adeline's children was, or whether or not he was the same person for both. No guesses, no inklings, no suspicions, a complete blank in Adeline's life. Mary believed firmly that Christina knew more than she was willing to say.

Paramount among the questions for Mary was why Adeline decided to give her five-year-old up at the time that she did, nearly two years after giving up Richard. Adeline's circumstances were not good, but neither had they changed during that time. She continued to live in the lighthouse with the McIntoshes same as before, and went with them after they moved out of the lighthouse. And, since Mary was never legally adopted by the Gallants, despite using that name from the day she arrived, how was it Dolph could simply say no to sending her back to her biological mother? And, again, why didn't Adeline come with Christina to the farm that day?

After all these years, the answers were hollow and disappointing: "times were hard," "best under the circumstances," or "no one

121

really knows." The truth, Mary suspected, was a complicated mix.

Christina did tell Mary that she had an uncle still living in the area, Adeline's only brother, Peter Whitty. Ultimately, Mary and Fred met and developed an ongoing friendship with Peter, although he too either wouldn't provide or genuinely did not know the answers to most of Mary's questions. He did, however, give Mary the one and only clear picture that existed of Adeline as a young woman.

Since her childhood, Mary had always strained to form in her mind an image of the woman who was her biological mother. Now, that actual face stared back at her from a formal pose, head and shoulders in black and white, and, to Mary's great surprise, the woman she saw was a complete stranger. All those years, Mary believed that somewhere within her the memory still existed, that she would only need reminding of those features, just a prompt, and it would surely come back. It did not.

Mary could see similarities between herself and her mother, the dark hair, the high cheek bones. But the overall shape of Mary's face, her eyes and especially her pointed nose, were not shared by her mother or any of the Whittys she had met. Those must have been inherited from her biological father, a man whose identity would remain a mystery.

Mary's biological brother, Richard, however, might be within her reach. Inquiries into the orphanage in Charlottetown had come up empty, just as Father Steele had predicted, but months later she received a call from a Father Elois Arsenault, the priest for the Immaculate Conception Catholic Church where Richard was married. Father Arsenault was responding to her written request for information. The priest told her that Richard Whitty went by the last name Nelligan and that he had indeed been married at the

Immaculate church. Further, Richard was still living in Tignish, and that he and his wife had six children.

Father Arsenault was confident they were talking about the right person because he was the priest who had convinced Richard to file that copy of his marriage certificate at the church where he was baptized. Father Arsenault had no reservations: he was happy to give Richard's contact information, and, he assured Mary, Richard would very much want to meet her.

In November, for the second time that year, Mary and Fred boarded the ferry to PEI. This time they would be travelling west to Tignish. After half a century, Mary would finally meet her brother, and he would meet the sister he never knew existed until her phone call. She couldn't wait to tell him all that they had done to find him, to show him the picture of their mother, and to relate everything she had discovered about their biological people, and about the family he now had in her, her husband, and their children.

"But when I got there, I couldn't say anything," Mary recalled. "We just stood and stared and stared for the longest while, and then we hugged and hugged. It was too hard to talk."

Mary assumed he would be short, like herself, which he was. He resembled their mother and the Whittys in general more than she did, but he was her brother, of that there was no doubt.

Their first day together flew by, although there would be others, many others: she and Fred in Tignish, Richard and his family in Pictou. Over time, Mary's and Richard's individual lives unfolded to each other.

Richard had spent much of his childhood in Mount St. Vincent's Orphanage in Charlottetown. During the Depression there were many orphaned children on PEI, many as a result of the highest tuberculosis death rate in the country. During the worst of the epidemic, PEI was the only province without a fully publicly funded TB Sanitorium. Finally, in 1938, one provincial TB sanitarium was built near Charlottetown, although priority had always been given to those who had a fighting chance at survival. The others were on their own.

In many cases, the Catholic Church, primarily the Sisters of St. Martha, not only tried to fill the severe health care gap on PEI, but they also became largely responsible for the Catholic children the disease and pervasive, gripping poverty left in its wake. Prince Edward Island, at the start of the Depression, already had very little wiggle room economically, with already the lowest per capita income in Canada during the first part of the twentieth century. Not many families were in the position in the 1930s to take on extra and so it was left, to a significant degree, to relatively few religious organizations to care for thousands of people in various forms of extreme need.

With a hugely reduced charity dependent income, however, Mount Saint Vincent's Orphanage itself was not much better off financially than the desperate people who required their services. The sisters grew their own food, for the most part, begged for coal, and budgeted everything else to the absolute minimum, poor as the proverbial church mouse.

Although the orphanage did its best to provide early education for between fifty and eighty-five children per year, one teacher for the girls and one for the boys, Richard never did learn to read or write functionally. At age eleven, he was taken in by the Nelligan family near Tignish. The Nelligans were very good to him and Richard loved them deeply. He liked being part of a real family, and when he left as a young adult, he retained their name, passing

124

it on to his own children. He spent most of his working life on the water, fishing, or in the woods, lumbering.

Richard, too, had always wondered about his blood relatives. How many did he have and would any be interested in meeting him? What happened to his father and mother? At the suggestion of his priest, he approached St. Mary's Catholic Church after he was married. But at that time, they either could not or would not tell him anything more than that his birth mother, Adeline Whitty, had died. The nature of Richard's existence was much different than Mary's. From the beginning until the day he and Mary met, Richard had been a living secret.

The officials at St. Mary's assured him, however, that his records would be there if anyone came looking. Mary did, and by the end of the process, she knew for certain the Gallants had saved her life.

29

SIR ROBERT

On a cold Saturday night in February 2016, Mary wiped her kitchen table for a final round of cribbage before Bob and his long-term partner, Oritha, had to go. Most of the Pictou crowd, including Fred, had opted for a hockey tournament in Halifax. They wouldn't be back until late, giving Jackie, down from New Brunswick for the weekend, an opportunity for a quiet catch-up visit.

Bob and Oritha needed to get home, though. Oritha had her grand-kids arriving for the night and Bob seemed tired. In hindsight, Jackie recalled him getting up from the table that late afternoon, and, just for a second, steadying himself on the back of the chair. If she hadn't known better, she might have thought he'd had a swig or two. But that couldn't be. Bob had not had a drop of liquor for more than thirty years. It had been the answer to Mary's most fervent prayers.

In the intervening years, since Mary and Fred moved back to Pictou, their family had expanded by leaps and bounds, with fifteen grandchildren, three step-grandchildren, and nineteen great-grandchildren. There had been the usual ups and downs every large extended family experiences, relationship struggles and job and money issues, as well as more than one serious illness. Bob had struggled the most and for the longest.

More than thirty years prior, in his thirties, Bob had hit rock bottom hard, his alcoholism on a whole other level than his father's had once been. In the end, for Bob, there was nothing remotely "functional" about his addiction. Practically every waking minute of every day involved drinking.

After Cathy, his first wife, took the kids and returned to Pictou, the last sliver of control Bob had been clinging to slipped from his grasp altogether. He ended up discharged from the military. He returned to Pictou, but, still drinking, couldn't hang on to a job any longer than a few months. Woman after woman came and went in his life, and his two still-young children suffered, confused and hurt by their father's erratic and unstable behavior.

Toward the end of a decade of escalating self-destruction, Bob found himself in the midst of yet another failed relationship, but this time another child was involved, a baby girl, and when her mother left, taking this baby too, Bob's descent was complete.

Fred found his oldest son sprawled and incoherent in the living room of his rented house, the smell of stale booze and whatever else rank in the room. Fred cleaned him up as best he could, practically carried him to the car, and drove him directly to the Detox Centre.

Bob never drank again after that, although the road to recovery was long and painful. Managing day to day was less about trying to cope without a crutch, and more like trying to walk without legs.

He married again, impulsively and mistakenly, the fallout from that added to the list of other problems the years of turmoil had created. The uncertainty of his income and finances was ongoing between changing jobs and accumulated child support, all of it compounding the strain of trying to stay sober and rebuild broken relationships, especially with his two oldest, now young adult, children.

127

During those early days Mary watched as the strength of Bob's sobriety grew in painstaking inches, as he fought for every bit of ground gained, and she was fanatical about trying to help him. Unlike his father, Bob did go to Alcoholics Anonymous and found tremendous support there.

Despite their different routes towards the same goal, Fred could relate more than anyone in the family as to what Bob was going through and the end of Bob's drinking marked the beginning of a genuine friendship between himself and his dad. The two men enjoyed each other's company, in the woods hunting or on the water fishing, and eventually their relationship reached the point where they could laugh out loud at the crazy antics they each had gotten up to, individually or together, in their drunken stupors.

Later on, Bob and Fred shared an old fishing boat, plugged, painted, and tinkered to sea-worthiness, its annual spring launching a celebratory occasion for them both. The *Jackie Lee Anne* they christened it, Fred supplying most of the money, "Sir Robert giving most of the orders," Fred liked to say, only half-joking.

Without the booze, the chaos in Bob's life eventually did calm. Finally, he met another woman, Oritha, who also had a painful past. Of all Bob's women, and there was never any lack of them, even in the worst of times, his relationship with Oritha was the most successful. They had similar outlooks, they approached life in similar ways, and while she was nobody's push-over, Oritha was able to handle Bob's impatient and quick temper better than anyone.

Bob had also found the job of his dreams, "farming" trout, part of Nova Scotia's inland fisheries management. He had taken an Aquaculture Technician program and landed a job at the Fraser's Mill Fish Hatchery near Antigonish. Basically, Bob got to go fishing every day, even most of the winter. He knew everything there was to know about the various kinds of trout, their beginning to end life cycles, their biology and habitat needs, and their natural numbers and re-stocking efforts throughout the interior of NS. And he also got to talk about it, to any and all interested members of the public, including a few not so interested.

The work satisfied Bob mentally and physically like no other had, and even approaching sixty-five, Bob had no intention of retiring any time soon. Contentment had come to him, and Mary discovered a measure of truth to the idea that a mother is only as happy as her unhappiest child.

On that particular winter Saturday night, after Bob and Oritha had left for home, Jackie was making a fresh tea for her mum when the phone rang. It was Bob's oldest daughter, Nadine.

"Where's Grampy? I can't get anyone," she cried into the phone. "Dad's here at the Aberdeen. They don't know what's the matter. He doesn't know us."

Apparently, Jackie managed to understand, Nadine had called her father that evening. Oritha had put the two grandkids to bed for the night, and gone downstairs to find Bob on the phone. Neither she nor Nadine, however, could make any sense of what he was talking about, his speech was so confused and jumbled. In a panic, Nadine raced to her father's house and convinced him to go to the hospital. Oritha would meet them there as soon as her own daughter came for the kids. The hospital was five minutes away, but by the time Oritha arrived, barely half an hour later, Bob had no idea who she or anyone else was.

Nadine finally reached her grandfather on the road from Halifax. He and the other family members among the hockey go-ers detoured to the hospital in New Glasgow. At home, Jackie knew

129

how intensely worried Mary was. She had retreated to her quietly serious mode, responding to Jackie's ongoing prattle by polite remote.

"Maybe it's his high blood-pressure, Mum," Jackie wondered, hope mixed with apprehension. "They should be able to get a handle on that though, especially getting to the hospital so quickly. Maybe what they call a TIA, a kind of mini-stroke. You know, what with his blood pressure problems, Mum."

Eventually, Jackie too went quiet. Finally, lights from the SUV flashed through the porch windows and tires crunched the frozen snow. Fred and his granddaughters filed into the house, the girls letting him take the lead. He went directly to Mary and took her by the shoulders.

"It's not good," Fred said, looking straight into her eyes, his dark complexion grey. "A brain tumour."

As it turned out, Bob had four brain tumours, the largest one behind his right eye, causing most of his immediate symptoms. They were "glioblastomas," the deadliest kind of brain cancer: fast growing, inoperable, untreatable.

Over the course of the next few days, Bob's confusion lessened, but physical impairments developed in a mushrooming slow motion, spreading gradually outward from his left side.

Bob and Oritha struggled for five months, the two of them arriving at Mary's and Fred's daily for tea or supper, refusing to give up whatever routine Bob could manage for as long as he and Oritha could cope. Eventually, he was admitted to palliative care, but Oritha's exhaustion only increased as she tried to be by his side every minute of every day and night, unable to rest at all in the hospital. And she knew that he would prefer to be home. She took him there and with Nadine's help, along with the occasional home-care nurse, she looked after him until he died, three weeks later, July 2, 2016.

For Fred, the pain of watching his feisty, strong son grow old in front of him, dependent and helpless, was unbearable. "It's not natural," Fred reflected, fighting to hold himself together and to make sense of the unfathomable. Within weeks of Bob's death, Fred sold the *Jackie Lee Anne*, the sight of it too torturous to endure.

During Bob's last months, Mary's outlook was different. As long as Bob drew breath she would carry on. Each day he lived was another day that she was able to move herself through time, one foot in front of the other. The alternative was simply not endurable, the idea that she could somehow go on after letting go of her child forever defied any realm of possibility in her mind. But, of course, Bob did pass, and Mary did go on, for another nine months.

30

ANOTHER END

Once the Palliative Care Unit's double doors softly closed, Jackie felt the hectic hustle of New Glasgow's Aberdeen Hospital transform into an oasis of quiet. Here, the staff never appeared rushed or stressed, and each of the unit's six private rooms were spacious and comfortable, large enough to accommodate a group of visitors during the day, or an overnight guest on a converted recliner-bed.

It was late March 2017, and Mary was in her ninth month of a knock-down, drag out battle with pancreatic cancer. The disease had been diagnosed less than two months after Bob died.

Jackie had come to give her oldest sister, Lee, an overdue break and not for the first time she wondered how Lee managed it all these months. Lee had been her mother's primary caregiver: night after night, week after week, month after month, either at the house or here at the hospital, in a roller coaster struggle that strangely mirrored Mary's completed life. It was emotionally and physically exhausting, and there was no denying, in sheer determination, Lee was her mother's daughter.

On this, the second night, Jackie was sleeping soundly, despite the uncomfortable bed, until she became aware of a tugging, a movement at the bottom of her cot. It jostled her awake enough to hear a raspy voice repeating her name along with the words "get out." She thought she was dreaming, but sat up, and was shocked to see her frail mother on the floor in the dark, the tips of her fingers stretched to grasp the covers at the end of Jackie's makeshift bed.

Mary had not been able to walk or sit up on her own for nearly a month. She weighed seventy-five pounds and could barely raise her arms. The effort to speak above a whisper seemed beyond her. Yet, there she was, trying with every ounce of strength she had left to save her child from a fire.

Of course, there was no fire. After Jackie punched the emergency button and the nurses rushed to the room, they managed to assure Mary that the scorched odour she was smelling was only a bag of popcorn left too long in the staff room microwave. They checked her over thoroughly, nothing broken, and re-settled her into bed. They apologized for scaring her, and marveled at the little woman's incredible strength of will.

"Yes," Jackie had to agree, "she is amazing."

Within weeks, however, the excruciating inevitable did come. On that last Sunday morning, for some inexplicable reason, Fred insisted he and Jackie would go to an earlier Mass at a church neither had been to before in Stellarton. Afterwards, they hurried over to the Aberdeen hospital. Uncle Winston, Mary's youngest brother, was already there, surprised at Fred's unusual change in his hard and fast routines.

Mary was still sleeping, he reported, hadn't opened her eyes since he arrived, and so he and Fred went to the unit's family kitchen for coffee. Jackie would meet them there after making a call from the unit's quiet room. On the way back up the hall, she sidestepped into her mum's room first for a quick peek. There she saw her mother wide awake, as alert as Jackie had ever seen her, though Mary's frail body was so weak only her eyes could follow her daughter's face as she came around the side of the bed.

133

"Mum?" Jackie said, leaning in, pulled by the strength of that stare. She grasped the bones of her mother's wrist, and the two of them held there like that, as if seeing each other for the first time, until Mary closed her eyes and stopped breathing.

Mary Elizabeth Whitty Gallant LeBlanc died on April 2, 2017 at age eighty-seven.

EPILOGUE

After both Mum and Bob were gone, when our losses were far enough behind us that it was possible to reminisce and smile too, we took comfort in our family's common cache of memories. As time passed, we again laughed at things no one else found funny and rehashed stories only we could tell. Our memories held the uniqueness of us, like a fingerprint.

Near the top of that long collection was one of the last times we had all been together at once, including Bob. It was summer vacation. "The raisins," as he referred to Mum and Dad, now in their mid-eighties, were staging what had become a nearly annual event, the slideshow.

They were among Mum's most precious treasures, those slide pictures, especially when viewed in a blistering hot, dark, and completely cramped Heights living room. Featured were old black and whites from their earliest days, continuing on all the way to the vibrant colour of their most recent ones: Germany, Oromocto, the kids, the faces so unbelievably young, the weddings, the exes, grandchildren, and now great-grandchildren.

Most of us assembled that night, however, were there less for the "slides" and more for the "show," the images already burnt into our memories from having seen them so often.

This performance began with the usual setting-up struggle between Mum and Dad. Pictures were taken down and furniture rearranged in order to gauge the optimum viewing angle. As usual, Mum settled on the one Dad originally suggested.

Predictably, somewhere near the start, Dad launched into his standard complaint about the "last dime" he had spent on the ridiculously expensive projector bulb, the one "Humpty-Dumpty" sent him all the way to Truro to retrieve. The bulb was years old by then. Humpty-Dumpty was his current nickname for Mum, who had broken a small bone in her foot. It was a step up from her previous title, "fossil." As was the custom, Mum and Dad positioned themselves behind the ancient projector and bickered over the fact that the machine was sticking, or that Dad was moving along too fast, or lingering too long, or he had, again, inserted the slides incorrectly so they appeared on the wall upside down or sideways. This time, Dad argued, it wasn't him who had gotten the slides ready for tonight's viewing.

The two of them took turns narrating. Dad provided hypnotizing details on things like a scene of sand somewhere in the Middle East, dotted by an army buddy in the distance. Mom described, or guessed, dates, homes, occasions, babies, children and/or friends, while Bob shouted one-liners, mocking any and all old-style clothes, hair-dos, pets, and spindly Christmas trees.

At last, on this night, came the final slide. It stuck partway through and Dad had to give it a bit of a shove until it showed clear and full. Everybody peered, but nobody remembered this one. Mum adjusted her glasses and Dad leaned in. It was a very young Mum, apparently, but where? Oh my God, not in the bathtub? Was that Mum in a tubful of bubbles, smiling at the camera, and, holy God, was that a left nipple splashed across the wall, magnified by a thousand?

"Fred," Mum screeched in a pitch high enough to break glass, "get that out of there." Dad was already frantically trying to do just that, but the slide was stuck, the carousel was stuck, and he

136

kept jostling it back and forth to unhook it, the image flashing on and off, on and off. "Jesus Christ, Mary, I can't get it out. Unplug it, unplug the goddamn thing," Dad yelled while Mum frantically hobbled her way the length of the cord to the outlet, gimp foot and all. Afterwards, Dad demanded to know where in hell and who in hell found that slide. Someone was damn well snooping around. Who put it in there? No one confessed, it was a while before anyone could speak, we laughed so hard.

Looking back, that had been such a revealing memory for us all, aside, of course, from the obvious. They had been so full of life, Mum and Dad. They had lived deeply and with such a simple richness, despite the tremendous ordeals they had gone through—most especially our mother.

From the beginning of her life to the end, Mum met challenge after challenge with an unwavering determination and commitment to her family. The reward and the proof of it were in that living room and on that wall that night. She had adapted, endured, and survived with love and laughter, music, a stoic denial of the hardships, and the kind of strength we, her children, hope exists within ourselves.

On a cloudless summer morning in July 2017, Mum's ashes, and some of Bob's with her, were buried in the Stella Maris Roman Catholic Cemetery in Pictou. There, along the shaded tree line, surrounded by four generations of people for whom she had devoted her life, our orphaned Island girl was laid to rest.

Someone once said that the value of memories is not in what we remember but why we remember it. This book is for my family. No words can express how grateful I am for our story.

-Jackie Muise